# Kent's Own

## THE HISTORY OF 500 SQUADRON ROYAL AUXILIARY AIR FORCE

ROBIN J. BROOKS

FONTHILL

Fonthill Media Limited
www.fonthillmedia.com
office@fonthillmedia.com

First published 1982
This revised edition published 2014

British Library Cataloguing in Publication Data:
A catalogue record for this book is available from the British Library

Copyright © Robin J. Brooks 2014

ISBN 978-1-78155-322-0

The right of Robin J. Brooks to be identified as the author of this work has been asserted by him in accordance with the Copyright, Designs and Patents Act 1988.

All rights reserved. No part of this publication may be reproduced, stored in a retrieval system or transmitted in any form or by any means, electronic, mechanical, photocopying, recording or otherwise, without prior permission in writing from Fonthill Media Limited

Typeset in 10 pt on 13 pt Sabon LT Std
Printed and bound in England

# Contents

|    | Acknowledgements | 4 |
|----|------------------|---|
|    | Foreword | 5 |
| 1  | A Squadron is Born | 7 |
| 2  | Prelude to War | 24 |
| 3  | From Manston to Detling | 29 |
| 4  | Blitzy Days | 40 |
| 5  | Operations Continue | 48 |
| 6  | The Detling Raid | 54 |
| 7  | From Detling to Bircham Newton | 61 |
| 8  | Ansons to Blenheims | 70 |
| 9  | U-Boat Days | 77 |
| 10 | Overseas | 86 |
| 11 | The Italian Job | 99 |
| 12 | Desert Air Force | 112 |
| 13 | Baltimore Days | 126 |
| 14 | Peacetime Operations | 139 |
|    | Commanding Officers of 500 Squadron | 155 |
|    | No. 500 Squadron Standard | 156 |
|    | Squadron bases | 157 |
|    | Bibliography | 159 |

# Acknowledgements

I acknowledge with gratitude and thanks all the people who have assisted me with memoirs, personal papers and photographs: Miss Daphne Pearson GC; Mrs Ann Griffiths; Group Captain D. Keddie; Group Captain D. M. Candler; Wing Commander H. N. Garbett; Squadron Leader J. W. Jarvis; Squadron Leader C. D. Pain; Flight Lieutenant R. Rogers; Flight Sergeant John Thompson (for his diary); Jack Hoskins; Stephen Cunningham; A. D. Cummings; Geoffrey Cardew; W. Keppel; G. Clinch; Russell Adams; K. P. Meehan, Doctor G. H. Templeman, and all members of the Kent Aviation Historical and Research Society. My thanks go also to Paul Grundy for the illustration of the squadron crest and the various line drawings throughout, and finally to members of 500 (County of Kent) Squadron Old Comrades Association.

# Foreword

I have long felt that with so many histories written about our county, one should have contained the story of our own auxiliary squadron. None did, so I was inspired to make amends.

From the beginning I did not intend it to be the story of the squadron from a strategic point of view, I leave this to the historians of our time. I wanted to approach it from the human angle, the despairs and the triumphs of the Men of Kent, Kentish Men and the Maids of Kent who served with 500 Squadron. With this book I hope I have achieved it.

I dedicate it to the men and women of the squadron who did not come back.

Robin J. Brooks
October 1981

A 500 Squadron Virginia flies over Kent.

Bombing up a Vickers Virginia J.7718 F/O Knapp, LAC Bates at the front gun.

# 1

# A Squadron Is Born

'*Quo Fata Vocent*'—'whither the fates may call'. The badge—a horse forscene—the prancing white horse of Kent, seen on and in various places throughout the county of Kent. It is the symbol of Kent and it is appropriate that the Latin inscription and the white horse should be brought together in a badge to represent the county's own Royal Auxiliary Air Force squadron—No. 500.

The battle honours for the squadron are numerous, among them the Channel and the North Sea, 1939–41, the Atlantic 1941–42 and Italy 1944–45. These are just three theatres in which the squadron has seen action. *Quo Fata Vocent* never seemed more appropriate.

The beginning saw the squadron receive the privilege of bearing the first number ever allocated to a Special Reserve squadron. It was actually the thirteenth of the 20 Special Reserve and Auxiliary Air Force part time units to form into a single unit but it received the first official number—500.

The units came together at Manston on 16 March 1931. The first commanding officer was Squadron Leader S. R. Watkins AFC, RAF and the adjutant was Flight Lieutenant T. B. Prickman RAF. On 4 June the squadron received the first of three Vickers Virginia bombers and two Avro 504N trainers. The Mayors of Margate and Ramsgate paid a visit to Manston to congratulate the squadron and to name the first Virginia 'Isle of Thanet'.

With the unit firmly established, Squadron Leader Watkins left and Wing Commander Forbes MC, RAF arrived to command. With this new officer an extensive recruiting campaign began. The idea was to present the new squadron to the people of Kent in the hope that it would encourage the Men of Kent and Kentish Men to join the already established unit of regular officers and airmen. By the middle of August 1931 it was apparent that there was a deal of enthusiasm amongst the inhabitants of Kent. Not only was the squadron growing in manpower, the equipment was growing as well!

On 5 October 1932, the aircraft in the squadron increased to six with two Virginias in reserve. The two Avro 504 aircraft remained as the basic trainers. The fact that the increase in aircraft was seen to be a sign that the new squadron was being accepted, gave even more encouragement to the Kentish people. So much so that by 12 November 1932, a paid weekend camp was held and was attended by five Special Reserve officers and 54 reserve airmen.

On 1 January 1933, the strength of the squadron increased to eleven regular and seven reserve officers, 77 regular and 52 reserve airmen. The aircraft strength remained at six Vickers Virginias and two Avro 504Ns. By May it was possible to send a good representation to the annual camp at Tangmere in Sussex. Tangmere was a relatively new aerodrome, similar in size to Manston. Here the newly formed squadron was able to take a fake operational role and it took part in many bombing exercises. On 1 June, two Virginias were transferred from No. 502 (Ulster) bomber squadron to join the six aircraft already operating with the squadron. The flight commander Squadron Leader T. F. W. Thompson DFC took three aircraft, six regular officers and six air gunners to the annual practise camp at Catfoss on 9 June and Wing Commander R. Halley DFC, AFC took over command of the squadron when Wing Commander Forbes was posted to RAF Netheravon.

Returning to Manston, the squadron co-operated with territorial searchlight companies who were at annual camp at the station. These exercises were invaluable both to 500 and to the searchlight crews. They had an air of reality about them, with the early rumblings that were evident in Germany, the personnel felt that it was for real.

The first tragedy of the squadron took place on 16 September 1933. Flying Officer L. M. Few, a Special Reserve officer, was flying Virginia K.2680 over Weybridge when he crashed and was killed. The cause of the crash was unknown. He was buried with full military honours, both regular and reserve personnel providing a guard of honour.

The same day Flight Lieutenant L. G. Nixon was posted to the squadron to take on the job of adjutant, his predecessor Flight Lieutenant Prickman being posted to No. 30 (Bomber) squadron stationed in Iraq.

The second accident of the squadron, according to a report in *The Times* took place on 18 February 1935. A Virginia had taken off from Manston and when approaching 500 feet above the ground, was seen to be on fire on the starboard wing. The flame was soon approaching the fabric of the fuselage. The pilot, Flight Lieutenant Morison made a quick turn and side-slipping to keep the flames away from the fuselage, lost height and landed up-wind. The three occupants jumped from the Virginia which was now enveloped in flames. The ground crews ran to the aircraft with fire extinguishers thus making sure that the aircraft was not wholly destroyed.

The first award came to 500 Squadron on 6 May 1935 when Corporal Charles Marsh, a special reservist, received the King George V Silver Jubilee medal. Wing Commander Halley was posted to the Fleet Air Arm on detachment and Wing Commander G. M. Lawson MC, RAF was appointed 500 Squadron commanding officer.

Summer camp, Tangmere, 1936.

A 500 Squadron Virginia airborne from Manston.

*Above left:* Avro 504N at Manston, 1936. (*W. Keppel*)

*Above right:* Summer camp. Ford, 1936. (*G. Cardew*)

Hawker Hart K3053, Manston, 1936. (*G. Cardew*)

500 Squadron Virginia at Ford Aerodrome. (*Richard Riding*)

A burnt out Vickers Virginia after a bomb blast. (*G. Clinch*)

Manston camp *c.* 1934. (*G. Clinch*)

500 Squadron. Annual camp, Tangmere, 1937. Flying Officer Anderson forgets to check his ballast. (*J. Wilson*)

The Royal Review that year took place at Mildenhall in Suffolk. 500 Squadron had the honour to appear before King George V and the Prince of Wales who were accompanied by His Royal Highness the Duke of York, himself an RAF pilot. (The Duke of York later became King George VI). The Vickers Virginias of the squadron flew past the King in formation and the personnel, officers and airmen, were inspected by his Majesty.

5 December 1935 came and the squadron converted to Hawker Harts, thus becoming a single engined day bomber squadron. With the situation in Germany now becoming more and more evident, the squadron was fully transferred into the Auxiliary Air Force on 10 May 1936. The County of Kent Territorial Army and Air Force Association assumed responsibility for the unit and the squadron was again re-equipped with the Hawker Hind. This was a two seat light biplane bomber which was accepted lovingly by the flying personnel of 500 Squadron.

With the arrival of new aircraft, Flight Lieutenant P. H. Dunn came to take over the duties of adjutant and in August 1938, whilst the squadron was at annual camp at Ford in Sussex, Air Commodore J. C. Quinnel DFC, air officer commanding No. 6 (Auxiliary) Group carried out an inspection of the squadron.

During his visit it was announced that His Royal Highness, the Duke of Kent, KG, KT, GCMG, GCVO had agreed to be the squadron's first honorary Air Commodore. The firm connections with Kent were beginning to take shape.

21 August 1938 saw the squadron back at Manston after a very successful camp. The Special Reserve or Auxiliary contingent of the squadron was by this time, moulding together and becoming a firm and formidable unit. So much so that the

Ground training—harmonizing sights on a Lewis gun/Cookhouse fatigues at summer camp, 1935.

Annual camp at Filton, 1936. Flying Officer Keppel's aircraft. (*J. Wilson*)

Summer camp, 1935. Centre is C/O Wing Commander R. Halley, DFC, AFC. Left is Adjutant, Flight Lieutenant L. G. Nixon. Right is Squadron Leader G. M. Lawson, MC. (*Kent Messenger*)

Summer camp. Ford, 1935. Squadron Leader C. G. Hohler maps out the day's flying. (*Kent Messenger*)

## A Squadron is Born

500 Squadron Hawker Hart over Kent, 1937. (*Kent Messenger*)

AOC's inspection, Ford, 1938. (*J. Hoskins*)

Flight Lieutenant A. C. Bolton, MC, led the advance party from Manston to Detling in 1938. (*W. Keppel*)

The advance party arrive at Detling from Manston, September 1938— Flight Lieutenant A. C. Bolton in centre. (*G. Cardew*)

Special Reserve men were taking commissions in the RAF. On 8 September Pilot Officer D. C. Jones was appointed to a commission in the Auxiliary Air Force with effect from 13 May 1938. He was one of several to receive a commission before a signal was received by the commanding officer of 500 Squadron, that the unit was to leave Manston for Detling, a grass airfield perched high on the North Downs and commanding a view over the Medway and Thames estuaries.

Flight Lieutenant A. C. Bolton MC took an advance party from Manston and proceeded to RAF station Detling on 14 September 1938 to prepare for the arrival of the main bulk of the squadron. A station headquarters had just been set up at Detling manned by a small nucleus of regular RAF personnel.

The station was a grass-surface airfield situated 600 feet above sea level. Though subject to hill fog, Detling was an ideal flying situation with good dimensions. North to south reached 1,035 yards, north east to south west 1,250 yards, east to west 1,014 yards and south east to north west 1,026 yards. There were no permanent obstructions and the airfield was in service for full operational use. Hangar accommodation was available for 500 Squadron's aircraft and there were 48,000 gallons of aviation fuel in store. To Flight Lieutenant Bolton's mind this was the ideal situation for a growing squadron.

With the deterioration in the international situation and the tension prevailing, orders were received to move the entire squadron to Detling earlier than it had been planned. The move was arranged to be effected from 3 October but this was now brought forward to 28 September 1938. On this day the main body and the aircraft of the squadron arrived at the station and the move was completed in twelve hours. Such was the urgency of the situation.

## A Squadron is Born 17

Detling in 1946—
unchanged from 1939.

The Hawker Hinds of 500 Squadron. (*P. Berry-Ottaway*)

The squadron soon settled into Detling and now, having taken residence at the station, began a routine of training that they had not experienced before. The Hawker Hinds were now seen over the estuaries even more frequently.

During October, three Hinds of the squadron provided air co-operation by day for an Air Raid Precaution demonstration at Faversham and the annual inspection of the squadron was taken by the Air Officer commanding No. 6 (Auxiliary) Group, Air Commodore J. C. Quinnell DFC.

The auxiliary squadron now received some of the semi-permanent officers posted into its midst. The Reverend N. R. Carmichael was appointed Chaplain (C of E) with the relative rank of Squadron Leader and in November, Flying Officer E. C. Gross LMSSA, was appointed to a commission in the auxiliaries (Medical branch).

1938 came to an end with the squadron now very firmly entrenched in part time active duty. Christmas was white that year and the regular personnel cursed their luck at having been posted to the station. The airfield froze, the water pipes iced up and the primitive stoves for heating in the buildings were totally inadequate. No running water was available for the airmen, it all had to be brought from a central tap, nowhere near the mess or their billets! The grass runways were covered in ice and snow allowing no flying but plenty of 'snow shovelling' exercise for the poor airmen.

January 1939 came and saw the strength of the squadron standing at three permanent officers, eighteen auxiliary officers, 65 permanent airmen and 163 auxiliary airmen. This month also saw many officers posted into the squadron for administration duties. On 20 January Flight Lieutenant G. A. W. Garland attended an armament and gunnery course at No. 1 Armament School, RAF Manby. This officer was instructed to pass on all the knowledge he gained at the course to the many auxiliary officers now in 500 Squadron to prepare them ready for the affray that everyone now believed would surely come.

The squadron was now classed as a general reconnaissance unit and Flying Officer R. E. Mack was posted to 500 as an instructor in reconnaissance. Two days later, Flying Officer Pat Green and Flying Officer Bill Kepple were sent on

Avro Anson—1939—500 Squadron. (*W. Keppel*)

detachment to Thorney Island to attend the first auxiliary air force navigation and reconnaissance course. That same day Group Captain R. L. G. Marrix DSO, Air Officer commanding No. 16 Group carried out the very last peacetime annual inspection of the squadron.

Rumours began to abound with the news that 500 Squadron was to convert to a new aircraft. It was generally known that it was to be a twin engined type but which of the new generation of aircraft was it to be? 19 March 1939 provided the answer when the squadron began to re-arm with the Avro Anson Mk. 1.

A development of the civil Avro 652, the Anson first flew on 24 March 1935. With glazing all along the roomy cabin, the aircraft was powered by Armstrong Siddeley Cheetah VI engines driving two blade fixed pitch propellers. With a capacity for carrying a bomb load and fitted with machine guns, the Anson carried a crew of four. The simple airframe was of mixed construction, the thick (originally flapless) wing being wooden and the rest being nearly all welded steel tube with fabric covering. On 6 March 1936 the aircraft entered RAF service with 48 Squadron, curiously enough, at Manston. Now it was the turn of 500 to receive a fairly modern monoplane.

Conversion to the type began immediately. Flying training and the knowledge needed to service the Anson was paramount in importance. On 26 March an Anson provided air co-operation by day for the Bearsted post of the Observer Corp, which had just been put on a war footing. This period was not however without its humorous times. As well as converting to the new aircraft, new equipment was being put into use at Detling. Much of it was a source of mystery to the regular and auxiliary personnel and many amusing incidents took place. Stephen Cunningham, then LAC No. 812142, told me:

Mayor of Maidstone (Councillor P. Brown) inspecting personnel of 500 Squadron in 1939. (*Kent Messenger*)

Blondie Bowers was a Corporal in the signals section in the year before the war started and he acted as an instructor to wireless operators under training. He was a regular serviceman and though somewhat disdainful of auxiliaries, he was well liked.

In early 1939 as a prized award, the station was supplied with a sectional radio mast comprising four 12 foot lengths. Blondie Bowers addressed in detail his class of auxiliaries who were to assist him in the erection. The mast was to be supported by guy wires at each quadrant.

At about this time, Corporal Bowers was replaced by another Corporal whose sense of humour was somewhat less. His geometry did not seem quite consistent with the problem, refusing all suggestions from his class, he outlined his scheme which relied on teams of 3 men at each quadrant, each man holding a guy with constant movement to follow the elevation. His plan appeared hopelessly complicated.

We were duly assembled for the erection with a growing audience of airmen, much to the pride of the new Corporal. The task commenced somewhat shakily and as the mast gradually rose the team had great difficulty in maintaining its line. Orders poured from the Corporal as the 'kinky' mast soared until suddenly the creature went out of control.

Anticipating carnage the last order from the Corporal was 'run', and 12 men scattered in radii whilst the mast collapsed into twisted debris.

500 Squadron was now transferred to the control of No. 16 (General Reconnaissance) Group of Coastal Command. Maidstone, the county town of Kent, marked the freedom of the town given to 500 Squadron on 6 May 1939 when the squadron marched through the town centre, the Mayor, Councillor Percy Brown, taking the salute.

Two weeks later, the squadron showed their strength and prowess at Detling to a crowd of 15,000 air minded people who turned up for the Empire Day Air Display. Many of the serving members and the public who came to see them knew that this was to be the last display of peacetime.

On 7 August 1939 500 Squadron attended its last peacetime camp. The officers, men and equipment were at Warmwell in Dorset. Sir Kingsley Wood, the then Secretary of State and Marshal of the RAF, Sir Edward Ellington GCB, CMG, CBE paid informal visits to the squadron. Talks were given to the personnel relating to the 'rape' of Czechoslovakia and the unrelenting tide of the German forces. With Europe now taking the German Chancellor's attention, the talks were of preparation for total war.

The squadron returned to Detling on 13 August and on the 25th came the signal that everyone had been expecting. Embodiment into the RAF proper and active service. The strength now stood at six regular officers, 28 auxiliary officers, 135 regular airmen and 320 auxiliary airmen. The squadron had fourteen Ansons, three Tutors and one Hind trainer. Ground equipment comprised Albion 30 cwt lorries and Crossley 3 ton lorries, together with a fire tender and ambulance. The fuel bowsers and trailers, plus a Cole's crane completed the squadron strength.

## A Squadron is Born

Empire Air Day poster, Detling. 500 Squadron took part. (*G. Cardew*)

Warmwell 1939. John Baldry learning to fly in the Avro tutor—Roy O'Nion leaning on wing. (*J. Hoskins*)

On 23 August the Germans and Russians signed a non-aggression pact, and German troops prepared to invade Poland. The squadron was immediately brought to instant readiness and 25 August 1939 saw the peacetime Operations book of 500 Squadron closed. John Thompson, then Aircraftsman 1st Class, explained:

> In August 1939, the pot, which had long been simmering began to come to the boil and all territorial and auxiliary service units were called to the colours. The first to be called up were anti-aircraft units and members associated with the hitherto unknown 'radar' sections.
>
> Ever since the Italian invasion of Abyssinia, we had been constantly on the alert and beset by innumerable alarms and excursions. This being so, an armourer mate and myself decided to go ahead with our long planned holiday at Butlin's holiday camp at Clacton, in direct contravention of our warning orders.
>
> When the recall telegrams eventually reached us at Clacton, we were already 'adrift' with all the possible dire consequences! We hastened home and collecting our kit, hurriedly made our way to Detling, where we were met by an atmosphere of frenzied but actually well organised activity.
>
> On booking in at the gate I was told I would be accommodated in hut C1 on the floor. Space was at such a premium that it was a case of one man on a bed and others

'Up front' on an Anson, Detling, 1939. (*Kent Messenger*)

500 Squadron fitting shop, Detling, 1939. (*Kent Messenger*)

on the floor beside him. I was also told to consider myself under 'open arrest' for reporting in late.

At this time, 500 Squadron had only recently passed from Bomber Command into Coastal Command and had been re-equipped with Avro Anson aircraft. One of the ground crew's first tasks was to ensure that each aircraft had its engine covers, pickets and the full schedule of equipment so as to make it largely a self-supporting unit.

I was in 'A' flight and our war dispersal point was on the top of Detling hill, near the little lane which runs down to the 'Black Horse'. At that time the edges of the field and the lane were quite heavily wooded with trees and bushes. We had to hack alcoves in the wood to accommodate and hopefully, to obscure our aircraft from the air.

Full of energy and enthusiasm, I assailed the unoffending chestnut trees with vigour. At this point a very junior officer approached me and enquired from where I had obtained the axe I was waving with such gusto. When I admitted that I had removed it from my aircraft, I found I was on my second charge since being called up!

The long prophesied war had come to Detling and to 500 Squadron.

# 2

# Prelude to War

To Ann Tebbutt and Pamela Thorpe the news that the war had been declared meant that their past training and lectures in the 19 Company (County of Kent) WAAF had not been in vain. They were now to be on active service.

Ann had become interested in the Air Force about the time of the Munich crisis in 1938. She walked into the local Army recruiting office in Maidstone, and to the horror of the recruiting sergeant, she announced that she would prefer to join the Air Force. 'You want the other end of the town for that lot,' choked the sergeant. Not to be put off, Ann went to No. 57 London Road, which was then the recruiting centre for the Air Force, and enlisted in the 19 Company WAAF, an offspring of the Royal West Kent Regiment.

She received her number, 882009, and was told to await a letter confirming her appointment within the unit. Some time was to pass until finally Ann and Pamela, who had also preferred the Air Force, joined the unit in May 1939. Group Officer Miss Cope, still wearing her khaki uniform though now the WAAF officer in charge, welcomed the 25 female personnel that made up the nucleus of the first WAAF establishment attached to 500 Squadron.

Gas and drill lectures were now held at the Royal Air Force drill hall, Astley House on the Hastings Road, Maidstone. It was much to the consternation of the men attending these lectures that they had to share them with their female counterparts. Ann Griffiths, née Tebbutt, told me:

> We used to attend one anti-gas lecture every week at Astley House. We used to wonder just what the men thought when they saw us coming into the room. I remember how hideous we all looked in those dreadful masks, not at all glamorous.
>
> I think the final straw for the men came when our WAAF officer told us we were so good at drill that Flight Sergeant Smart of the RAF, intended to put us on the square to show the men just how to drill properly, and to teach the newer recruits how it was all done. I wonder now, how he felt in drilling a squad of female recruits in civilian clothes.

## Prelude to War

Astley House also saw lighter hearted moments. The house was used socially as well as for the purpose of training people for the advent of war. Jack Hoskins remembers:

> I recall a time at Astley House when a show was arranged by Pilot Officer Van Damme, a member of the theatrical family. At some expense he arranged for the Windmill girls to come to Maidstone on a Sunday night when they were not performing at the Windmill theatre in London. There was a clamour for tickets as soon as news got round that a troupe of 'scantily clad' females would be performing in the house.
>
> The performance however, ended in up-roar. During the performance, whether or not by excitement from the male audience, a fire extinguisher was knocked over and proceeded to spray us all. The curtain rang down rather rapidly on the show and 500 Squadron.

Two days after the peacetime Record of Operations Book for the squadron had closed, mobilisation orders were sent to the 25 girls in the Kentish WAAF. It was announced on the radio that all personnel should report to their units post-haste. Ann Tebbutt and Pamela Thorpe, still dressed in their civilian clothes, reported to Detling.

Arriving at the station they found that the squadron had already arrived and was settling in. Now came the job of documentation and finding the girls duties.

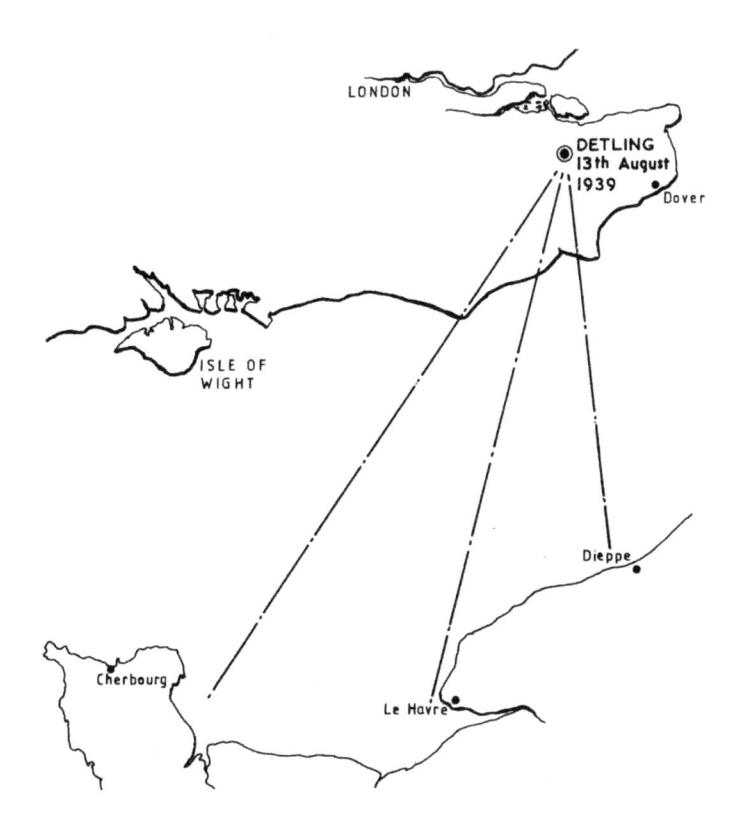

When we joined up we did not have any trades as such. When the officer in charge asked us what we wanted to do, I was so keen that I just wanted to shout: 'Oh, I'll be a cook!' Thank goodness I did not, when later on that day I saw just what a cook had to do in primitive conditions.

Eventually Ann and Pamela went into the telephone exchange. They were each issued with arm-bands, no uniforms were yet available. The girls were encouraged to take air experience flights in the squadron aircraft during August and September 1939. Arrangements were made by the Station Commander that any WAAF who wished could be taken up when the opportunity arose.

I well remember sitting in the co-pilot's seat of an Anson, operating the bomb switches when told to by the pilot. We would fly over some part of Kent where we could see sheep in the fields. They were then taken for targets and we practised 'dive-bombing' on them.

The living quarters for this 25 strong band of girls were situated in some cottages that were on the edge of the airfield. Known as Binbury Cottages, they were far from idyllic. They had no heating save a coal fire, and the early winter of 1939 was one of the worst on record. The WAAFs froze! There were two to a room and the end cottage had to serve as a mess. The cottages were tiny inside and very uninsulated. The wind and snow seemed to creep in everywhere. So cold did the girls feel that Ann's father drove with great difficulty up the icy Detling hill with her eiderdown and hot water bottle from home. The water tower on the camp froze which entailed

Medical staff at Detling sick bay, 1939. Back row: Cpl Hart, LAC Stone, LAC Ford, LAC Yaxley, Sgt Thomas. Front row: LAC Corner, Corporal Daphne Pearson. (*Daphne Pearson*)

Card depicting cookhouse staff, Detling, 1939–1940. (*G. Cardew*)

Astley House in 1981. This was the 500 Squadron training centre in 1938–39. It is situated on the Hastings Road in Maidstone. (*Author*)

filling the kettle with snow to get enough hot water for her hot water bottle. The same water went back and forth until the thaw came! Even the Air Ministry noticed the cold, and orders were sent down that every girl was to be issued with an Airman's overcoat. However, so short was the supply at that time, that a coat was issued only on the strict promise that it was to be handed in when the recipient was posted from Detling. When Ann finally left Detling in February 1940, her grandfather took pity on her and bought her a new coat to wear at her new station. Eventually the issue to WAAFs consisted of a raincoat and beret, but this did not happen until the end of 1939. Uniforms were short and the 'Phoney War' was just beginning.

Joan Daphne Mary Pearson joined the Women's Auxiliary Air Force around the same time as Ann and Pamela. The daughter of the Reverend Henry Pearson, she hailed from St Ives in Cornwall, having the profession of a photographer. She suffered from varying health in early life and moved to Kent to take up a less exacting and complete change of job. Her interest in the countryside and the lure of a job in the fresh air bought her to a fruit farm in Kent. She chose to work in East Malling, and lived in a house at nearby Ditton. The change of environment made sure she remained in fairly good health and she then joined the 19 Company WAAFs. She became one of the 25 girls that joined 500 Squadron.

Daphne Pearson wanted to fly with the auxiliaries. Weekends had seen her frequently at Ramsgate Airport, helping and flying whenever she could. She learned to fly, or almost! Unfortunately war broke out when she only had a few hours to do to gain her private pilot's licence. In 1939 however, it was not permitted for women to become aircrew and so, rather grudgingly, she chose the medical section and became the first woman medical orderly. She did not know that at this time, fate had taken a hand and was leading her on to, in her own words, 'a little something', whilst the Battle of Britain raged overhead.

All the girls who had joined initially had now arrived at Detling. Various duties were allocated, telephone duties for Ann and Pamela, medical for Daphne and administrative and operations room duties for many others.

Around the airfield, the Army had arrived to man the ack-ack defences by day and by night. Many of the aircraft were moved out to dispersals and posters appeared in the messes warning of the dangers of talking too much. War had come suddenly to Detling and the WAAFs of the squadron were ready to do their part.

Miss Cope, WAAF, C/O, Detling, 1939–1940.

# 3

# From Manston to Detling

I am speaking to you from the Cabinet Room at No.10 Downing Street.

This morning the British Ambassador in Berlin handed the German Government a final note stating that, unless we heard from them by eleven o'clock that they were prepared at once to withdraw their troops from Poland, a state of war would exist between us . . .

I have to tell you now that no such undertaking has been received and that consequently this country is at war with Germany. Now may God bless you all. May He defend the right. It is the evil things that we shall be fighting against—brute force, bad faith, injustice, oppression and persecution—and against these the right will prevail.

On Sunday 3 September 1939, the men and women of the squadron heard those words by the Prime Minister, broadcast on the radio at 11.15 a.m. For many seconds no one spoke, each person left alone with his and her own thoughts. Thirty minutes later two Ansons were taking off with orders to patrol the immediate area. No one knew whether or not the Germans would immediately attack the country. That very day a new Record of Operations Book opened for the squadron:

DETLING 3.9.39—11.15 hrs. WAR DECLARED BETWEEN GOVT OF GT BRITAIN AND NORTHERN IRELAND AND THE GOVT OF GERMANY. 12.00 hrs.—Aircraft to carry bombs on all future flights.

17.09 hrs.—Five aircraft to carry out parallel track search.

Included in this first patrol of the war was the aircraft of Pilot Officer Armstrong. The crew consisted of Sergeant Hoskins, LAC Bishop and LAC Wilkins. The duty report read as follows:

Anson MK-N.—Duty—Leave base—time up 08.46—time down—11.03. A/c reports escorted *Monn's Queen* from Boulogne at 09.10 hrs to Dover at 10.35 hrs. 2 fighter escort.

Convoy consisted of 12 MV (motor vessels) and 1 DR (destroyer) at MFDM 5535 at 09.45 hrs. Weather—Viz 20 miles, cloud 2/10ths cirrus approx. 1,600 ft increasing to 10/10ths over Kent coast at 4,000 ft. Sea moderate.

As it was the Luftwaffe's onslaught did not materialise and the days dragged lazily on. The Phoney War had arrived. John Thompson told me:

The squadron largely had to work under orders from the Admiralty as so many operations were based on maritime exigencies. This led to a lot of difficulties, particularly for the operation controllers and aircrews. The naval mind, used to manipulating vessels with weeks of duration, never seemed to fully comprehend that aircraft, with their comparatively small fuel supplies, had only one way to go when they ran out of fuel. Down! Several crews were lost trying to regain base after staying out longer on patrol over a convoy than was really safe.

Then there was darkness and the blackout which blotted out many landmarks, and of course, the fog which encompassed Detling at frequent intervals. Sometimes crews were unable to locate the field quickly enough when their fuel was low. They either crashed or force landed in the surrounding territory.

A spare Anson perspex rear turret was mounted on top of the camp water tower and an unfortunate 'erk' was posted there, complete with a pair of binoculars and a field telephone. It was his responsibility to warn of approaching raiders and to give the 'aerodrome raid imminent' signal. On receipt of this, and only then, personnel were allowed to cease work and take to the shelters.

During this 'phoney' period, always present was the threat of invasion and attack by paratroopers in the guise of 'nuns'. My flight commander, a shy diffident man, but a very good officer and pilot, was the proud possessor of a vintage 'De Dion Bouton' car and also a smart Bentley. At his instigation, we fabricated and welded up a couple of light metal mountings to take a Vickers 'K' machine gun.

On an occasional quiet evening, the flight commander would approach me and suggest it might be a good idea to go hunting for parachutists. Nothing loath, we would pile four or five lads aboard and with the guns mounted and armed, off we would go on our intrepid patrol. Diligently we would search in all the bars of the 'Black Horse' and the 'White Horse' at Bearsted, and finally the 'Cock Horse' at Detling, with meagre success. Forays north to the 'Wheatsheaf' and the 'Three Squirrels' were considered too reckless, as these areas were the haunts of the ruffian 'B' flight personnel and they couldn't be relied upon to observe the tenets of the Hague Convention.

This period of non-activity by the enemy came as a very welcome relief to not only 500 but the military forces as a whole. It allowed more concentrated training and more tactics to be experienced. It also gave the powers that be, more time to find many loop-holes in the system. Jack (then Sergeant) Hoskins told me:

Gas defence practice, Detling, 1939. (*W. Keppel*)

An Anson patrols a convoy in mid-Channel. (*IWM*)

John Baldry and I were probably the only two Leading Aircraftsmen who flew on operations as co-pilots. We were soon hastily granted our wings and promoted to sergeants without taking the exam or the flying test—probably to cover up the 'clanger'. I did my first mission with Flying Officer Pat Green as captain on 13th September 1939. How lucky we were that there was a phoney war period in which to gain experience.

The main task of the squadron was reconnaissance operations over the Channel and in the Dover Straits together with convoy and single ship escort work. The fuselages of the Ansons had been painted green to blend in with the colour of the sea. In addition to a bomb load, the aircraft had a Vickers machine gun that fired through the nose and a single Lewis gun that was set in a dorsal turret.

The war was only two days old when the squadron made its first mark on the history books. Anson 5066 was on patrol together with 5051 in the Channel approaches. Piloting 5066 was Squadron Leader Crockart with Flying Officer Keppel, Corporal Wanstall and AC2 Coomber as crew. The pilot of 5051 was Flying Officer Green with Flying Officer Maby, LAC Walton and AC2 Rodgers as his crew. Coming down just below the fleecy cloud, Flying Officer Keppel noticed an enemy submarine, apparently stationary, and on the surface. Wheeling round, and noticing that the submarine was about to dive, Squadron Leader Crockart dived and dropped his bombs in the vicinity of the vessel. By the time the Anson had turned round for a machine gun run the submarine was submerged. Anson 5051 began to position for a run-in but it was too late, no sight was seen of the enemy. Both aircraft patrolled the area for a time but no wreckage or oil was observed. Running low on fuel, both aircraft returned safely to Detling achieving the honour of being the crews to make the first air attack of the war. The Record of Operations Book for the squadron proudly states the fact:

| Aircraft Type and No. | Crew | Duty | Time up | Down | Remarks |
|---|---|---|---|---|---|
| ANSON N.5066 | S/L Crockart<br>F/O Keppel<br>Cpl Wanstall<br>AC2 Coomber | ATTACK a | 12.55 | 14.50 | Suspected Aluminium marker. VDSV 5613. |
| ANSON N.5051 | F/O Green<br>F/O Maby<br>LAC Walton<br>AC2 Rodgers | ATTACK | 12.35 | 14.19 | No sign of Submarine. Weather reported by both a/c to be fine, visibility 20 miles, sea smooth. |

'B' Flight at dispersal, Detling, 1939–40. Flying Officer Pat Green, Flying Officer Isles, Pilot Officer Wheelwright, Flying Officer Stockdale, Flying Officer Schreiber. (*W. Keppel*)

This first incident of real war helped to bring the reality of the situation to the squadron, for during this period, life still carried on much the same as pre-1939. Ann Griffiths told me:

> I remember we played hockey matches on the sports field. It really was unfair when you saw some of the larger members of the squadron up against us girls. One match I played in I received a tremendous knock on the knee from an opposing player. It absolutely crippled me, I fell to the ground in agony shouting 'ouch' and various words! This incurred several visits to the sick bay but the pain was alleviated by a surprise box of chocolates.

Detling was lucky to have a cabaret-cum-floorshow made up from members of 500 Squadron. The troupe called themselves the 'Robins'. This was a very accomplished cabaret group comprising fifteen male members of the squadron and seven female. The act was a self-contained band with singers and actors. As well as giving shows at Detling, Eastchurch aerodrome on the Isle of Sheppey was also visited and entertained. The entire equipment and cast were moved around in a 3 ton van, much to the consternation of the local constabulary who often turned a blind eye to such things as this during the early period of the war. It is not recorded whether or not any of this 'strolling' troupe went on to greater things in the form of music and drama!

The realisation of war was brought back to 500 Squadron on 9 September 1939 when a patrol nearly ended in disaster. Anson N.5052 had taken off from Detling

Pilot Officer Dennis Mabey, Pilot Officer Andrew Paterson, Pilot Officer Norman Harris, Detling, 1939.

The 'Robins' floor show, Detling 1939–40. (*Ann Griffiths*)

at 19.00 hrs (7 p.m.) for a search and reconnaissance patrol. The crew was Pilot Officer Bob Jay, Sergeant John Baldry, Leading Aircraftsman 'Schnozzle' Ridley and Leading Aircraftsman Steve Cunningham. It was a very fine dark night with little cloud. No Radio Directional Frequency facilities were available until a system of coding was devised, as it was believed that the enemy would use this information to their advantage. Thus the D/F stations were silent, and the crew had to rely on their own navigation.

Approaching over the coast at the end of the patrol, the aircraft was challenged by searchlights by the Army crews manning them. Appropriate colours were fired from the verey gun by the crew until, having been challenged several times, the verey cartridges were all used. The aldis lamp was further used to answer the searchlight and gun crews and this seemed to satisfy them. The Anson was now low on fuel and the continual challenging had taken the aircraft somewhat off course.

Switching on the landing light, Pilot Officer Bob Jay examined the possibility of a forced landing. Making one or two ground approaches in the pitch dark, he found the ground was most unsuitable, on one occasion missing a tree by what seemed inches. This persuaded him to abandon the attempt and to think about the next move. Stephen Cunningham remembers:

> Pilot Officer Bob Jay and John Baldry then huddled together presumably discussing their next move. John came back to Schnozzle and me and told us the outcome. We were to use available fuel to climb and in the meantime we should open the windows, put on parachute packs and prepare to jump when instructed. I think we all welcomed this outcome after the hairy approaches.
>
> All went to plan. There was difficulty in getting out with the 'Mae West' and pack on but we succeeded. Once clear of the aircraft I can remember the enormous peace and after pulling the rip-cord, the impression was, after the initial jerk and swinging, of being hooked in the air without movement. It was a delightful sensation.
>
> I landed in a field and after collecting my parachute and clutching it like a laundry bundle, I heard a call and walked towards it. It had come from Schnozzle, who was unhurt. We could make out some moving lights and found that our field abutted a road up which we walked, finding a cottage nearby. We called and were hailed from an upper window by a lady who seemed surprised when we asked her what county we were in. It turned out that we were near Wilmington and when the place had been named, we had asked 'near Dartford?' to be told that this was Wilmington near Eastbourne.
>
> We were invited in and our parachutes explained our predicament. The cottage had a telephone and so I reported to Detling, explaining just what had happened.
>
> A keen local ARP squad arrived shortly afterwards led by a Mr McCutchan who was a director of Harrod's Store. He was most helpful and took control of Schnozzle and me. The police had located the other members of the crew, who were taken to

hospital with injuries. Schnozzle and I were taken to Mr McCutchan's home and served with a meal and drinks. We were then accommodated for the night. I can recall the meal included an excellent steak washed down with a bottle of Vat 69, most of which was consumed!

In the morning a salvage party from Ford aerodrome collected us and took us to the aircraft which had fallen not too violently, into the River Cuckmere where it had become an object of great interest to the local residents. We were able to recover the camera and certain personal possessions.

There was a humorous postscript to this accident. One of the regular staff at Detling, Leading Aircraftsman Jock Buchanan, was by trade an electrician. By day and by night he was also a gambler. He would bet on anything and when the call up occurred and patrols commenced, he saw an opportunity to 'make a book'. Normal patrols which started from date of call up, before the war was declared, were of three or four aircraft and Jock's book was based on the proportion of aircraft that would return from each patrol. Stephen Cunningham again:

> It took him two days to get organised so that from about 26 August, he made a daily book but the consistent safe return of all aircraft night after night spoiled his venture so that in early September, he reluctantly abandoned his scheme.
>
> On 9 September, four aircraft went on patrol. I was in one which met with problems and, as previously mentioned, we had to bale out in Sussex. Returning to Detling two days later, one of the first people to greet me was Jock, with far more enthusiasm than was expected. He explained that four aircraft had gone out on that night and none had returned. At this precise moment, we realised that his joy was not unconnected with the prospects our experience had given him of reviving his 'book'.

The first aircrew injuries of 500 Squadron came on the same day as Pilot Officer Bob Jay's crash. Another Anson was returning from patrol when bad weather forced a crash landing on the sea off Whitstable. The crew were picked up by the Whitstable life-boat with superficial injuries and taken to Canterbury hospital.

September moved into October and the weather again did not improve. It hampered operations for the squadron and was the cause of many fatal crashes. Anson N.5233 was returning from patrol having escorted a convoy through the Channel. Over Benenden, on the approach to Detling, it developed engine trouble and began to lose height quickly. The order was given to abandon the aircraft and the pilot, Flying Officer D. G. Maby attempted to gain a little more height. Managing to reach the crucial level, Leading Aircraftsman Mesent baled out to safety. Unfortunately, no more of the crew had the opportunity to jump and Flying Officer Maby, Pilot Officer A. M. Paterson and Corporal J. F. Drew perished in the crash, the first fatalities of the war in 500 Squadron.

*Above left:* Flight Lieutenant Baxter in Detling Mess, 1940. (*W. Keppel*)

*Above right:* One of the first tragedies of the war in 500 Squadron. Pilot Officer Andrew Paterson crashed to his death on 7 October 1939 aged 29. He lies in Detling churchyard. (*Author*)

'A' Flight at the ready, Detling, 1939–40. (*G. Cardew*)

Bad landing—Avro Anson at Detling, 1940. (*J. Wilson*)

November saw the squadron keeping to the routine of photographing shipping and loose mine spotting off the English coast. The enemy became very curious about the activities of the Ansons seen over the Channel and occasionally came within the range of the guns of the aircraft. One advantage of the Anson with its slow speed, was that the enemy fighters overestimated how fast it was travelling and always shot straight past. This enabled the gunners to get in some shots which occasionally hit the enemy aircraft but always frightened them off!

On 10 December 1939, a crewman died from his injuries when another Anson crashed near Detling. Patrols were being carried out in appalling weather, resulting in very many crashes. One problem in flying from Detling was that the maximum run was only 750 yards, and the ground rose 100 feet from north to south where it dropped steeply away towards Detling village. When the wind blew from the southeast it was touch and go whether the Ansons would 'unstick' in time before hitting the perimeter and the main road. Some very experienced as well as the less experienced pilots came to grief on take-off when flying in that direction in bad weather.

The period of December 1939 through to January 1940 experienced the worst winter weather for many years. The rain and snow seemed never-ending. Whilst the aircrew of the squadron had problems flying, the ground crews and WAAFs. had their own difficulties. Servicing the aircraft became a major headache when tools froze to the ground and the fitters could not feel their fingers for the cold.

The WAAFs, in their quarters in Binbury Cottages, began to wonder what misfortune had brought them to Detling. With no water and insufficient heating in the cottages, life became a nightmare for them and many were glad to remain on duty just to keep warm. At least the offices and various sections in which they worked had reasonable heating.

As December now approached, many of the men and women of the squadron attempted to capture the Christmas spirit as best they could. After four months of war this was not an easy task. Though the full spite of the enemy had not yet been unleashed upon them, or upon Great Britain, they all knew that it would not be long before they would be subjected to full and total war. For two days in December, all of these thoughts were put aside as festivities took first place. Father Christmas arrived on board one of the squadron aircraft and both officer's and airmen's mess were decorated in tinsel and chains. Many felt that this was to be the last Christmas so spent, for who knew just what the next year would hold? Though no-one knew it, Detling was to be subjected to the real horrors of war.

# 4

# Blitzy Days

January 1940 arrived in the same fashion as December, snow and ice covered much of the country. Squadron Leader W. Lemay was promoted to command the squadron. A popular officer, he was to see the squadron through a very difficult period. During this month, the Ansons escorted the leave boats from France and the squadron took on the task of mine spotting.

The squadron gunnery officer at this time was Flying Officer Harold Jones. Fora long time he had been concerned about the Ansons' vulnerability in combat and was determined to do something about it. Obtaining the permission of the new commanding officer, he fixed two additional .303 machine guns to fire from positions along the fuselage side. This made the aircraft appear somewhat like a 'bristling porcupine' but it made the Anson a far more aggressive and lethal aircraft. The movements of our convoys in the Channel Straits encouraged the Luftwaffe into the air at every opportunity and it was not long before the extra firepower of the Anson was put to good effect. It was a great morale-booster for the squadron.

The ensuing months saw 500 supporting convoy movements, reconnaissance of the enemy lines and escorting boats from France across the Channel. The squadron flew 1,386 hours during the month of April, much of it in abysmal weather. Fighter and bomber activity from the Luftwaffe was increasing as the period now known as the 'Battle of Britain' approached.

On 15 May 1940 came a rare incident. A Heinkel 111 bomber was flying above Anson MK-B which was protecting a Channel convoy. Keeping station above the Anson, the Heinkel dropped his bombs in the hope of hitting the aircraft. Several bursts of gun-fire from the fuselage sent the enemy scurrying into the protection of cloud, no damage occurring to the Anson.

The squadron were now doing daily patrols over the coast of France as our soldiers tried to escape from Dunkirk. The aircraft attacked many German surface vessels trying to attack the armada of small boats and rescue boats picking up the men from the beach.

On 25 May, the Dunkirk evacuation proper began and there arrived at Detling an amazing collection of aircraft. Pilot Officer D. H. Clarke reported there for duty on 30 May flying a target-towing Blackburn Skua of No. 2 anti-aircraft co-operation unit stationed at Gosport. His orders were to patrol each night west of Dunkirk dropping powerful flares to light up any attempt by the German Navy to interfere with the evacuation.

Next morning, as his operation was not timed until after night-fall, he assisted the ground crews, some of them being 500 Squadron personnel, who were working on about 50 Fleet Air Arm Swordfish aircraft which were due to take off on a patrol across the Dunkirk beaches. The idea was that the Germans would think the Swordfish to be the equally obsolescent Gladiator fighter and would be frightened off by them.

The second patrol of the morning was flown by the aircraft of 500 Squadron with additional aircraft made up of Fleet Air Arm dive bombers and two-seater fighters. The additional aircraft consisted of 37 Skuas and Blackburn Rocs. Pilot Officer Clarke watched the return of the patrol just before lunch-time. He recalled:

> There were not many of the little fighters left, I counted six. One of them belly-flopped on the grass and I went across to see what had happened. The aircraft was a complete write-off. Bullets and cannon shells had ripped the fuselage from end to end, the after cockpit was sprayed with blood. The front cockpit was worse. Two bullet holes through the back of the pilot's seat showed where he had been hit and his parachute, still in position, was saturated in blood. The instrument panel was shattered and on the floor was the remains of a foot.

Of the original force of fighters, nine came back and five were written off on inspection. The remaining four aircraft were airborne within the hour. Clarke recalled: 'They looked very pathetic limping back to Dunkirk all alone.'

500 Squadron was now playing a significant hand in the evacuation. Three aircraft from No. 48 squadron were detached to Detling to assist the squadron with patrols over the French coast as our soldiers continued to escape before the might of the German Army arrived at the coast. The Luftwaffe too were around in force attempting to stop the evacuation and to clear the skies over Dunkirk of the RAF.

The overall command of air cover for the evacuation was in the hands of Air Vice Marshal Keith Park, the commander of No. 11 group, Fighter Command. The Hurricanes and Spitfires of Fighter Command could only patrol for forty minutes before they had to return to their airfields to refuel. The time between was taken up by a variety of other aircraft and squadrons including 500. Inevitably there were times when there was no air cover whatsoever. 'Where was the RAF?' was the accusation of bitterly tired men on the Dunkirk beaches. They knew nothing of the battles going on further up the Channel and the losses the RAF were experiencing. 500 Squadron was no exception. Anson MK-U crashed into the sea during a patrol, the crew being rescued by a destroyer, and MK-N failed to return from a mission on 29 May. Flight Lieutenant Richard Rogers told me:

Detling, 1940. (*W. Keppel*)

Pilot Officers Stockdale and Foster, Detling, 1939. (*W. Keppel*)

Detling 1940. Front row: Sgt Shier, Sgt Bachillier, Flt Sgt Wilson (in charge of 'A' Flight), P.O. Bob Jay, P.O. Keppel (Flt Comm), ?, Sgt Adams, Cpl Onion, Sgt O'Kelly, Cpl Wandstall. 2nd row—various including Priestly, W, Curtis, G. Springett, Wilson, Warburton, A. Thunoof, Starks, Bud Wilson, S. Longridge, Grist. Back row—various including Stitt, Wimhurst, A. Berry, D. Bussy, Tucker, J. Thompson, N. Munday, C. Etches. *C. Wilson*

Hon. Air Commodore HRH Duke of Kent with Squadron Leader W. K. Lemay on left and members of aircrew, Deting 1940. (*G. Cardew*)

The month of May proved a very hectic month. We were all very keyed-up and practically lived in our flying clothing, and seemed always to be in the air. We had hourly knowledge of what was happening across the Channel, being very much involved in it at first-hand and being chased home by enemy fighters. We were eating and sleeping at the dispersal area in requisitioned private dwellings. Often during the month I carried out two Ops trips in one day.

Dunkirk had fallen toward the end of the month and we were covering the evacuation. Several times we managed to avoid being shot down and got back home, but on the 29 we were attacked by a number of fighters at low level. The petrol tanks caught fire and we were pounded with bullets. Sergeant Hoskins, the pilot, pancaked the aircraft into the sea. I was thrown forward on impact and broke my left collar-bone and left shoulder.

The Anson was 5065 and we came down in the sea about seven miles off Dunkirk at twenty past six in the evening. The sun was shining and the sea was calm. Sergeant Hoskins, under heavy attack, skilfully brought the aircraft down not far from one of the many small ships that were bringing home the soldiers from the beaches. We were fortunate to be picked up by a tug, itself already laden with soldiers who were in all manner of distress, many of them badly wounded and burnt. Several of the soldiers, in a sort of half-crazed state, began firing with their rifles at the aircraft, sinking and nose-down in the sea with just the tailplane and rear part of the fuselage remaining above water attended by intermittent crackles and puffs of burning fuel as it slowly sank.

I was in considerable pain and also suffering from some shock. Moreover, having flown so much during the month I was, like most of us on the squadron, in a pretty keyed-up state. A kindly Petty Officer on the tug strapped up my shoulder and gave me some rum to drink. As my ribs were bruised and the straps were tight it hurt somewhat to breathe. However, my small troubles were as nothing compared to

Flight Lieutenant Tommy Dodds between patrols, Detling 1940. (*W. Keppel*)

many of the poor soldiers, some of whom were terribly wounded and had been on the beaches for days. During the night, in mid-Channel, I was transferred to a paddle-steamer, (the *Royal Daffodil*) and the following morning we arrived at Ramsgate, where among many other wounded servicemen, I was put in a church which had been converted to a temporary first-aid centre. From there I was sent to Farnborough hospital where I remained for six-and-a-half weeks. I had completed 35 operational patrols during the month.

I later learnt that my W/T SOS had been received by the powerful receivers at Manston and I was extremely pleased about this because when one is transmitting under attack it is very difficult to concentrate.

The struggle carried on for five days. Each evening saw many more thousands of troops returned to our shores. Many faces were missing from the mess at Detling when it was all over. Many aircrews were weary and utterly exhausted. Winston Churchill the Prime Minister said:

> Wars are not won by evacuations. But there was a victory inside this deliverance which should be noted. It was gained by the Royal Air Force.

The men of 500 Squadron could not agree more. Even now, although Dunkirk was over, there was no lull in the dangers for the squadron, or from flying from a major airfield.

The month drew to a close with Anson N.9916, piloted by Sergeant D. C. Spencer overshooting the landing area and coming to rest in the hedge. Whilst the aircraft was damaged, no casualties resulted.

As the end of the month approached, it fell to the women of the squadron to make a mark on the history books. One in particular was to be involved in what in her own words she described as 'a little something'.

On the night of 30–31 May 1940, several Ansons had taken off for the purpose of bombing enemy held harbours in France. Anson MK-W, serial No. R.3389, failed to release its bombs and turned back for Detling. As usual the bad weather had hampered the operation from the start. The crew of MK-W were Pilot Officer Bond, Flying Officer Chambers, Corporal Petts and Leading Aircraftsman Smith. Realising that the situation of landing with bombs still on board was highly dangerous, the crew prepared themselves for what they hoped would be a very soft landing.

Crossing the English coast, one of the Cheetah engines began to splutter and the aircraft began to lose height. The weather was closing in rapidly and the pilot, Pilot Officer Bond was doubtful if they would even find Detling. With a last gasp, the engine finally stopped. Through a break in the cloud, the crew were able to find that they were a few miles or so from the airfield and prepared for a crash landing. Approaching on the final turn, the stalled engine suddenly burst into flame. As the Anson lined up for the airfield, the other engine began to cut out having run low on fuel.

With a great deal of skill, Pilot Officer Bond put the aircraft down on the grass runway but it landed badly and began to slide across the surface. A bad crash landing was imminent as the flames spread across the wings and began to envelope the fuselage.

To Corporal Daphne Pearson, lying on her bunk in the Women's Auxiliary Air Force quarters, it was not unusual to hear the Ansons splutter a bit when returning from a raid. On this particular night however she heard and saw something that was terrifying and ominous. The medical section corporal quickly pulled on her clothes and wellington boots, seized her tin hat and ran out of the building toward the aircraft.

A dull glow identified it as she scrambled over a hedge, fell down an incline and over a slight bank until nearly at the burning wreckage. There she saw three men staggering around in a dazed condition.

'The pilot is still there, he's knocked out,' shouted one of them as they made for the wailing ambulance that had arrived on the scene. Too shaken to attempt to get him out themselves, they barely saw the slim form of Daphne Pearson run past them towards the burning Anson. There she found the pilot still strapped in his seat. Releasing him from his harness, she dragged him from the seat and pulled him clear of the burning fuselage. Regaining consciousness for a moment, the pilot murmured something about the fuel tanks and the bombs aboard the plane. Daphne then realised that at any moment the Anson would explode. With all of her strength, she pulled Pilot Officer Bond away from the aircraft and over the ridge that she had just fallen over. Placing him on the ground she put her herself on top of him to protect him, removing her tin hat and placing it on his head.

Pilot Officer Bond then murmured something about his face and she saw that it had a lot of blood on it and a tooth was protruding from his upper lip. She reassured him about his face and was attempting to remove the tooth from the wound when the plane went up with a tremendous explosion. They were only about 30 yards from the blast. But for the ridge protecting them from the splinters of metal and the shock wave, they would both have perished. So great was the blast that other helpers rushing to the scene were all blown flat on the ground.

The ambulance arrived for the pilot but only when she was satisfied that she could do no more did Daphne leave the scene of the accident. Completely un-awed by her heroic deed, she wrote to her mother in Cornwall stating that she had been involved in "a little something". 'My name has been sent to the King,' she said. 'But I hope nothing will be done about it. When I read of the things our boys did at Dunkirk my little bit is nothing at all.' The King however had different thoughts on the act and courage of this brave WAAF.

During the month of May, the squadron flew 1,286 hours. The weather had improved considerably but the dispersal areas were now extremely muddy and slippery rendering conditions somewhat hazardous for people working on the Ansons.

Usually the aircraft carried a crew of four, pilot, co-pilot, wireless operator and air gunner. The gunner was not trained in wireless procedure and always flew in the rear turret. The wireless operator flew in the wireless position at a desk on the port side, just forward of the rear turret, in the cabin. Now it had become necessary to mount the Vickers guns in the fuselage to fire from the port and starboard rear windows adjacent to the wireless operator's position. Wireless operators had therefore to be trained in gunnery. Flight Lieutenant Richard Rodgers remembers:

> I had learnt my trade of wireless operator initially at Cranwell as a boy entrant and then at the School of Air Navigation at Manston. Prior to my being posted to Detling, I had acquired 86 flying hours as a wireless operator on Anson aircraft.
>
> I was one selected to be trained in gunnery when the additional guns were fitted to the aircraft. I had, in fact, been training myself at every available opportunity. Somehow I had sensed that this was the way things were heading and in this way I had got to know about it all. The gunnery examination was held at Eastchurch and along with several other men from the squadron, I was successful. This meant that I received the air gunners' badge together with the appropriate rate of pay.

Ann Tebbutt, though shortly to be posted from 500 Squadron, received reminders of the problems and the struggle that the squadron had to endure in this opening stage of the war. Operating the switchboard or PBX as it was called, may have seemed an isolated job, far away from the turmoil and drama of flying and servicing aircraft, but she too played a big part and saw another side of the human drama. She told me:

> Something that would always upset me was when the tailor would ring Detling and inform me that a certain suit or uniform was ready for fitting or collection. I would take the call at the exchange and tell the tailor I would pass the message on. Sometimes however, that particular person would not return from a mission and I had to let the tailor know.
>
> At other times it was so sad to see a car, waiting outside the mess for its owner who had possibly crashed to his death or who was so badly injured he was not expected to live.

Happier moments too are remembered such as when a certain pilot would 'buzz' her parents' house at Bearsted to let her know that he had returned safely from a mission and that he would be calling for her later that evening when he came off duty. Then it would probably be off to the 'Tudor House' for a tea dance or perhaps a meal and a drink at the 'Royal Star' in Maidstone, both firm favourites with the squadron.

Now it was time for Ann to leave the squadron and her good friend Pamela with whom she had joined up. Taking her memories with her, she was posted to headquarters, Coastal Command.

# 5
# Operations Continue

1 June 1940 arrived and started in dramatic fashion. Anson MK-V piloted by Pilot Officer Phillip Peters was on patrol over a convoy in the Channel when it was attacked by nine Messerschmitt 109s. The co-pilot, Sergeant D. Spencer manned one of the side guns and Leading Aircraftsman Pepper the other gun. Again the enemy overestimated the Anson's speed and shot straight past. Pilot Officer Peters hauled up the nose of the aircraft and fired the front guns. One of the 109s received a hit and dived into the sea. Leading Aircraftsman Smith in the rear turret scored another hit and a second enemy plane hit the sea.

Leaving the area rather rapidly, Pilot Officer Peters set a course for Detling. The news of the affray went ahead of his landing and upon arrival at the airfield he was welcomed by applause and cheering by many of the squadron personnel. When the ground crew inspected the aircraft, one bullet hole was found in the front section but no bullet. When Peters had his parachute repacked some time later, an intruder was found in the pack. One German bullet!

For this attack and for the morale-boosting effect on the rest of the squadron, the pilot was awarded the Distinguished Flying Cross and Sergeant Spencer, newly promoted Corporal Smith, Leading Aircraftsman Dillnutt and Leading Aircraftsman Cunningham received the Distinguished Flying Medal.

With the arrival of June, the squadron suffered numerous tragedies. On 14 June, Anson MK-M failed to return from patrol and on the 28 MK-E was seen to crash into the Channel, with the loss of all of the crew. Between these two losses, a further morale-booster helped the squadron.

Sergeant Prentice was the rear gunner of MK-N when it took off for a convoy patrol on 24 June. Arriving over the convoy of ships in the Dover Straits, the Anson took up its position. After about fifteen minutes of quiet patrol, the aircraft was attacked by several 109s. Positioning the Anson to allow the gunners to fire at the enemy, Sergeant Prentice sent several salvoes into the belly of a 109, having the satisfaction of seeing it crash into the sea.

July was a similarly depressing month. On the evening of the 11th three aircraft were detailed for a night patrol. It was a particularly foul night as the aircraft moved from the dispersals to the grass runway. Two of the Ansons successfully took off but the third, MK-F, piloted by Sergeant Wilson with Sergeant Shier, Sergeant O'Kelly and Sergeant Worton as crew, crashed just as it became airborne. The Anson landed in some woods about half a mile from the airfield. Tragically all of the crew perished in the crash, the bodies not being found until the next morning. Squadron Leader C. D. Pain recalls:

With regard to Sergeant Wilson's crash in 'F', I remember the occasion very well as I was Orderly Officer that night, and went to search, with others, for the wreckage and bodies. The woods in the area of the crash were covered in fuel, which kept igniting, and we could find no recognisable pieces of the aircraft, nor at this time, any bodies. The bombs had exploded on impact. Sergeant Shier had been my navigator from Dunkirk time until this very trip.

The accident happened on a night take-off at about 23.45 hours. The weather was appalling and the cloud was right down on Detling Hill. The first two aircraft, piloted by Pilot Officers Norman Harris and John Lane respectively, took off and climbed up

Wireless Op/Air Gunner Sergeant O'Kelly, crashed in Anson MK-F, 11 July 1940—buried at Detling Church. (*G. Cardew*)

through the cloud. By the time they returned the weather had cleared sufficiently for them to make a dawn landing back at Detling.

Sergeant Wilson's aircraft crashed immediately after take-off. I heard the usual roar of two Cheetah engines and then a terrible explosion followed by dead silence. It was pouring with rain at the time and the aircraft probably hit a tree.

I can still remember poor Sergeant Wilson's BSA 'Scout' four wheeler sports car standing for a long period in dispersal before being removed. It was a sad business this 'mad' war.

The crew were found next morning, two of them being in a kneeling position amongst the scorched trees and grass. Sergeant Shier and Sergeant O'Kelly were taken for burial at Detling Church. Sergeant Wilson's body was taken for private burial in his home town of Ayr and Sergeant Worton was buried at Enfield, his home town.

The next night was again a bad one when Anson 'D' failed to return to base from a fight in which nine Heinkels attacked the squadron's aircraft whilst protecting a convoy in the Channel. Anson 'L' claimed one of the enemy and several Spitfires, coming to the rescue, shot down another one.

The crew of Anson 'L' were Pilot Officer Pain, Flying Officer Jay, Pilot Officer Bliss and Sergeant Oakwell. Taking off at 07.01 hours on 12 July, they joined the convoy in the Channel. The squadron diary for the period gives the account in very dispassionate words:

Aircraft joined convoy of 21 MV (motor vessels) and 2 DR (destroyers) at LSWT 1757. At 07.40 hours, course 190 degs, speed 10 kts. Escorted it to CPWT 4337 at

Heinkel 111 shot down by C. D. Pain and crew in an Anson, July 1940. (*C. D. Pain*)

11.00 hours. At 08.40 hours convoy was attacked by three Heinkels 111K. Anson climbed to intercept and found nine Heinkels in all at 6,000 feet. Anson shot down one Heinkel. Spitfires appeared and immediately attacked Heinkels with some success. MV Hornchurch was sunk during action and crew rescued by DR. Action was over at 09.25 hours. Visibility 15 miles. Cloud 4/10 at 4,000 feet. Sea slight.

This attack was no mean achievement.

With the arrival of 18 July 1940, Anson 'G' was on convoy patrol when again the enemy turned his might against the squadron. Again the crew were successful and shot down a Messerschmitt 110 which was menacing the convoy below. At this time the mountings for the unofficial guns that were placed along the fuselage of the aircraft began to work loose. With the constant vibrating and recoil from the firing, the mountings became very unsafe and would have caused injury to the airmen manning them. As a gesture for the fine and dangerous work that the squadron were engaged in, Tilling-Stevens Ltd of Maidstone manufactured a more substantial and safe mounting and presented it to the squadron as a gift.

On 19 July a change of command came as Wing Commander C. H. Turner took over 500 Squadron. The Ansons were still maintaining a vigil over the convoys and suffering heavy losses. Some incidents, however, managed to lighten the gloom of the war. A. D. Cummings told me:

This is the story of a certain 'erk', who shall be nameless. Being a bit of a lad-about-town, he went into Maidstone one evening to keep a date with one of his many girlfriends, this time masquerading as a pilot.

His girlfriend was much impressed to find her new found hero was wearing two pairs of RAF pilots wings, a pair over each breast pocket. Being a rather observant type of lass, she asked why he had gained such a distinction. He replied: 'I am the pilot of a twin engined bomber!'

Again one evening a certain corporal went out on the town at Maidstone suitably attired, wearing an officer type collar (Van Heusen) and shoes. Strolling round the town waiting for opening time, he was apprehended by a couple of patrolling military policemen for being improperly dressed. He was asked to accompany them to the local headquarters at Wrens Cross.

En route they passed the Granada cinema, where he was granted permission to pop in to contact his friends to cancel the evening's arrangements. He duly returned to his patiently waiting escorts, thence to the headquarters where he was formally charged with being 'improperly' dressed.

The corporal promptly denied the allegation, now having unbuttoned his great coat to reveal a properly dressed NCO, boots and all.

It was at this point that the military policemen realised they had been so cleverly tricked. Whilst in the cinema, the airman had changed certain articles of clothing with his mates. The charge was cancelled and he was given his freedom, plus some very dirty looks! The corporal went along to a pre-arranged pub to celebrate the victory in great style with all those who had aided and abetted.

During July the Marshal of the RAF, Lord Trenchard, visited the station to talk to the men of the squadron and to see them in action. A hurried flying show was arranged and Detling was made thoroughly 'spick and span' for the occasion. Arriving early, Lord Trenchard took lunch in the officers' mess, leaving the station at midday.

July rolled on. The weather was now high summer. The Germans were making final preparations for the coming onslaught on Britain. The dawn of *Adler Tag* (Eagle Day) was approaching. This was the plan to annihilate the Royal Air Force, making the way clear for an invasion of Britain, code-named 'Sealion'. Dawn was early and sunset late. Well before it was light, the crew-rooms were resounding with the noise of telephones and flying boots thudding on the floor. Outside the weather was cold and clear and the aircraft sat patiently drying off the morning dew in the first rays of the early sun. Coming out from breakfast, a few of the pilots surveyed the sky trying to feel just what the day would bring them. For some it was to be another day to live, for others death.

The dummy airfield of Detling was Lenham, a gliding airfield of some proportion just between Harrietsham and Charing. The idea of a dummy airfield was that the

500 squadron over Dover harbour. (*Kent Messenger*)

enemy would mistake these minor airfields for the main fields in the south-east. Model aircraft of the right proportions were placed around the fields and mock hangars erected to, give the impression that it was a front line station.

For some time it had been noticed that enemy formations of aircraft would often fly straight over the field at Lenham when returning from a raid or directly over it whilst proceeding to a designated target area. Though no-one knew it at the time, this was early reconnaissance by the Germans for what became known as Detling's 'blackest day'.

As July came to an end and the Battle of Britain still raged overhead, the losses of the RAF became critical. Fighter Command were taking the brunt of the enemy's action, including the fighter airfields strategically placed in the south-east and known as No. 11 group. Coastal Command, of which 500 Squadron was a vital part, was also having its problems. Many of the aircraft were obsolete before the outbreak of war and posed little threat to the enemy's aircraft. The Ansons had a very hard task trying to protect the convoys and bomb enemy held harbours in France and Holland.

No respite was forthcoming as August arrived. Still the arduous duties of convoy protection, mine spotting and bombing were the order of the day. As the aircraft flew over the enemy coast, the aircrew could see the preparation for the invasion of England. Most of the harbours showed signs of barges and landing craft of all shapes and sizes. The sight of all this made the men of the squadron even more determined to prevent invasion at any cost. The freedom of our nation was at stake.

On Monday 12 August, grouse shooting began, as it had done for centuries. Not even war would deprive the country squire and landowner of this sport. If the records had said: 'Tuesday 13th August, Detling shooting and bombing began', it would have been most appropriate, for the worst day in the history of the airfield had dawned.

# 6

# The Detling Raid

Detling Operations Book—13 August 1940.
- 03.38— Air Raid yellow
- 03.53— Air Raid white
- 06.38— Air Raid yellow
- 06.48— Air Raid red
- 07.02— Siren sounded
- 07.41— All clear
- 07.43— Air Raid white
- 11.15— Weather—fair in Channel Straits and inland—cloudy with occasional rain or drizzle in the NW of the area. Cloudy over North Sea, Dutch and Belgian coasts. Patches of sea mist and haze. Outlook—cloudy in north, mainly fair in south.
- 15.53— Air Raid yellow
- 16.00— Air Raid red
- 16.05— Aerodrome attacked by German a/c. Severe damage caused including direct hits on the ops' room. There were numerous casualties and deaths.
- 23.10— Air Raid purple.
- 23.46— Air Raid end.

So states the records book in very dispassionate words. On Tuesday 13 August 1940 the Luftwaffe arrived to try to wipe Detling off the face of the map. It very nearly succeeded.

The station had been relatively quiet all day. Several air raid warnings were issued with the colour codings but none lasted long. That is until the warning at 15:53 hours turned to red at 16.00 hours. At this time precisely, eighty-six Junkers 87 (Stuka) dive-bombers appeared out of the cloud just approaching the airfield. This was Luftflotte 2 led by Hauptmann Von Brauchitsch, a recently decorated Luftwaffe hero.

## The Detling Raid

Shrieking from the cloud, the Stukas achieved the measure of surprise they needed. Many of the airmen and women on the airfield were taking tea in the mess when the first bombs fell. The accuracy of the raid was good. Every runway was hit, the length of them just bomb craters, rock and earth. Fires were started in all of the hangars eventually spreading to enormous proportions and rendering 22 aircraft destroyed. As the operations room disappeared in one large explosion, the Station Commander Group Captain Edward Davis, a former tennis champion, fell dead with a piece of jagged concrete driven straight through his skull.

As the Stukas spread death and devastation at Detling, the local population wondered just what had hit them, Casualty Clearing Officer Wallace Beale, a Maidstone undertaker, sped to the shattered airfield together with local units of the Civil Defence. The scene they found would have made many a weaker man ill. Of the 67 people killed, many needed only 5' coffins reserved for unidentified remains. A further 94 were injured and many of them could not be treated in the station sick bay. A fleet of ambulances arrived to take the badly injured people to Preston Hall hospital, there being not only air force personnel, but army as well. Several of the machine gun posts and the anti-aircraft sites situated around the airfield had received bomb hits and many of the men manning them were badly injured. Detling was a mess! The complete surprise of the attack had shocked the servicemen and women of the permanent staff and 500 Squadron. Squadron Leader S. W. Jarvis remembers:

On August 13th 1940 I was on the staff at the station headquarters at Detling which comprised a group captain commanding officer, a squadron leader administration, the adjutant, the assistant adjutant who was myself, and two junior WAAF officers. On this particular day the squadron leader 'A' was off duty and also the two WAAF officers. During the afternoon the C/O and the adjutant went together to the operations room, this left me as the only officer in the station headquarters.

Suddenly I heard the sound of an aircraft approaching at high speed and very low. Thinking that it must be one of our own planes returning to beat up the station after a 'kill', I was surprised to see the explosions of two 1,000 lb bombs on the roof of the operations room as I was walking across the room to look out. Fortunately, the window was shut otherwise I should probably have been killed by the blast as the explosions were only about 30 yards away. Just then the station RED air raid warning commenced to sound very belatedly so I rushed off to prevent any of the office staff from attempting to go to the air raid shelters whilst bombs were still falling and other aircraft were racing round shooting up the planes on the ground and anybody in sight. However, the station warrant officer, who like myself was a 1914 veteran, was already at the front door instructing everyone to get into the central passage and lie down on the floor or crouch down.

Now I must digress for a few minutes while I detail the main features of the air raid warning plan which had been in operation. We could hear the RED warning when it was sounded in Maidstone, but that was over four miles away and usually only a small number of aircraft came in our direction. By taking to our dugouts on every RED warning we were wasting far too many hours of working time every day, therefore it was arranged with the Observer Corps for them to phone us every time that enemy aircraft were coming in our direction and about two minutes flying time away. Then our own RED alarm was sounded and it was a standing order for everybody to stop work and dash off to the nearest shelter. Unfortunately there was nothing about what to do if the bombs were already falling before the RED alarm was sounded, that was why I rushed off so quickly to prevent anyone from going out. For the majority of the people on the station this was their first time in action, with nobody to restrain them they dashed wildly out to become casualties before they reached the shelters.

As soon as the station 'all clear' had been sounded ambulances were quickly on the scene where our two doctors joined them. One of the first things I did was to phone the operations room to enquire after our C/O and adjutant. I learned that they had been just below the spot where one of the bombs had fallen, the C/O was killed instantly and the adjutant had been blown along one of the passages and seemed to be in pretty bad shape and was being sent to hospital. It was ironical really as the operations room had been considered to be the safest spot in the station with a special bomb proof roof. The officers' mess was also very badly damaged putting it quite out of action and it was very nearly time for tea. I was the mess catering officer and was very pleased when the senior WAAF officer informed me that her girls had asked her to invite the officers to use the half of their dining room which was not being used by them at present. We accepted their kind offer with thanks.

After this I went outside to see how the station warrant officer was getting along with tidying up the wreckage, etc. The doctors had examined every casualty, the dead were left where they were, but where possible the others were moved to a convenient place to await the ambulances. It was necessary to collect the dead and line them up in a clear spot ready for the undertaker. As some of them were rather unsightly, I told the warrant officer that I would take that job over myself if he could find half-a-dozen men who were willing to assist me. We had no stretchers available as they were all being used for the living casualties therefore the dead had to be carried three or four men to each body as required. Some of the bodies had parts of their arms or legs blown off, we made a small pile of the oddments that we found and left it to the undertaker to sort them out if he could.

When we had finished transporting the bodies to a piece of land near the main gate we covered them all with blankets including the pile of oddments and departed to have a welcome hot drink in the dining room. We had left behind 36 bodies and one pile of oddments.

Soon after the raiders had all left Group headquarters rang up to ask what the situation was, a few minutes later Air Ministry rang up with the same question. Each of them was given a brief account and name of the senior wing commander who would act as C/O until a replacement was posted into the station. After this I returned to the orderly room to finish off the days work.

## The Detling Raid

Such was the devastation and death at Detling on this day. Squadron Leader Jarvis saw the death and destruction from the ground. Douglas Pain saw it from the air:

At about 7.30 p.m. on the evening of 12th August, the Detling air raid siren sounded off a RED warning. I remember walking out of the mess anteroom, out through the front door, casting an eye towards the nearest air raid shelter which was about 150 yards away in the direction of our 500 Squadron 'B' flight hangar.

At that period of the war a RED warning was sounded only if enemy aircraft were approaching and in the immediate vicinity, so that normal work would not be unnecessarily interfered with. So we knew what we might expect.

I heard the noise of enemy aircraft engines to the east, (quite unmistakable by anyone with an ear for that sort of thing) and there I saw what looked horribly like 'the chain' as it was known to the Spaniards during their civil war—Stukas going into line astern in a half circle over our adjacent 'dummy' airfield at Lenham. They made one or two complete circuits at a height of about 10,000 ft, their light blue under-surfaces glistening almost white against the deep blue sky. Then, to my amazement, they suddenly made off to the east. Shortly afterwards the 'all clear' sounded. I could only think that they must have been scared of an attack by our fighters, as they had no cloud cover.

Next morning we had to carry out a convoy anti-submarine escort patrol which necessitated flying to Bircham Newton in Norfolk, landing to refuel, doing a fairly lengthy patrol which meant landing back at Bircham to refuel again before returning to Detling.

We took off at about 06.30 hours and set course for the North Foreland, our usual sea departure point. The crew were: myself as pilot, Flying Officer Bob Jay—navigator, Pilot Officer George Bliss—air gunner and Sergeant Oakwell—wireless operator. There were cotton-wool balls of cumulus cloud forming at about 3,000 ft in a bright sky.

The old 'Anson' bumbled along. I said over the intercom, with what turned out to be remarkable prescience, 'Detling is going to catch a packet today'. No-one else spoke.

Our convoy patrol from Bircham was uneventful and we landed back there just in time to enjoy a really good lunch: The weather was glorious, and after lunch we lingered in the anteroom over a glass of port. Bircham Newton was famous for its food and drink.

We took off and flew back down the coast. Whilst over the Thames Estuary we found a wrecked ship and decided to have some front gun practice on it. I had shot down a Heinkel 111H with my front gun on the previous 12th June so we regarded ourselves as rather superior to Hurricanes, if not quite up to the standard of Spitfires! We then set course for Detling.

As we approached, the sky clouded over, 10/10ths at 3,000 ft. There also seemed to be something strange about the airfield. Scars of yellow earth all over the surface. Then the hangars—good God! They looked rather like badly damaged kitchen colanders. It was unbelievable that this could really happen to our home. It was most unfair! It was—it was war!

We sailed slowly round the circuit, noting the damage. The ops room had obviously taken a 1,200 pounder bomb right in the centre. All the messes had been blown to bits except the WAAF's dining room. We landed carefully, picking our way through the craters that covered the aerodrome, and taxied back to 'A' flight hangars and offices which were more or less in one piece. We had missed the whole show because of our dallying on our return. How lucky can you be!

We leapt out of the aircraft and made for the remains of the ops room. Here we heard that amongst others the station commander Group Captain Pat Davis had been killed and also Squadron Leader Oliver, one of 53 squadron's flight commanders. The rescue work was in full swing so we went to our various messes to sort ourselves out as best we could. A 1,200 pounder had landed slap in the middle of our anteroom, but on the edge of the crater stood our radiogram, quite undamaged and still playable. I remember that my beer tankard was the only one which was completely untouched amongst the mess silver tankards!

Another incident concerned our squadron commander, Wing Commander C. H. Turner. He was making a simulated blind approach under the hood, as it was called, in one of 'B' flight's Ansons, with Squadron Leader Pat Green sitting beside him as 'safety' pilot. Suddenly the whole airfield seemed to erupt in their faces. Pat Green whipped the hood from the eyes of the astonished 'Winco' who was presented with the sight of his squadron base being reduced to rubble. They opened up flat out and low and hastily landed at Rochester airfield a few miles to the north-west.

Flying Officer Harold Jones, our excellent gunnery officer, was doing an inspection of an Anson in 'A' flight hangar with one of his airmen. Suddenly bombs began to fall all around them. He said afterwards: 'You know, it was very strange. There were only two of us and one Anson in that hangar yet we kept running head on into each other.' I think this gives a good idea of the sort of thing induced by a sudden and unexpected blitz, even amongst well-disciplined men when caught off guard.

It was a case of the airfield being caught off guard. With the warning coming a little too late to be of any use to the people working at the time, the devastation was considerable. Apart from the warning that came from the sirens, an airman doing visual watch for enemy raiders also sounded the alarm too late. He was perched on the top of the old watch tower in a fort like construction. He sounded the alarm as the raiders flew over the field, felt very exposed up there so he shot down the steel ladder and made for the nearest air raid shelter. The shelter received a direct hit, killing all of the occupants inside whilst the watch tower was unscathed.

For the WAAFs at Detling it was a terrifying experience. Pamela Thorpe wrote to Ann Tebbutt who was now at headquarters Coastal Command:

I expect you heard of the awful raid of the 13th August. I was just leaving the ops block and posting a letter when suddenly out of a cloudy sky they swooped. There were about 50 or 60 'huns' and they let all hell loose. Never have I heard such a noise. I ran like fury with two airmen, they, poor dears got killed by bullets in the back as we were machine-gunned as we ran. I have never in my whole life been so utterly terrified.

I was hit by some flying wood so I threw myself on the ground while everything blew up as they dive-bombed.

All of 'B' flight went up including planes just near me. Afterwards I got cracking and cleared the road by the sick bay with my hands so that the ambulances could pass.

After that raid it has been continual, in fact we spent night and day underground and work went to blazes. Fortunately only one WAAF was seriously hurt. At last everyone had moved off camp and it is only used for flying, a damn good job! We are all billeted out, which is fine and we work 'somewhere in England'. The poor old WAAF quarters got somewhat bashed about, our new messing hut caught a packet and every window was smashed. I worked for 48 hours after the main raid without sleep and carried on with very little for three weeks and then got three weeks leave.

In spite of the hit on the operations room and the casualties, the WAAFs went on plotting the enemy in another building. Corporal Robins of the WAAFs was awarded the Military Medal for her courage some time after the raid. She was in a dugout by the operations room when it received the fatal hit. A number of men were killed and two seriously wounded in the same dugout. Though dust and rubble filled the shelter, Corporal Robins immediately went to the assistance of the wounded and rendered first aid. She fetched a stretcher and stayed with the wounded until they were evacuated. Another Military Medal was awarded to Sergeant Youle of the WAAFs as a result of her courage during the same raid. She was on duty in the station telephone exchange when it received a direct hit with other bombs in close proximity. The staff were subjected to a rain of debris and splinters together with a lot of glass. It was solely due to the cool bravery and the example set by Sergeant Youle that the telephone operators carried on with their task with calmness and complete efficiency at a most dangerous time for all.

As evening approached the situation at Detling became recognisable. Plans were made to evacuate the WAAFs and some of the non-essential personnel to outlying houses leaving just the duty and the aircrew people at Detling. The sick bay was moved out to a big house on the Sittingbourne road called 'Woodlands'. Further medical accommodation was made available in Nissen huts erected in the garden. The WAAF quarters were moved to a mansion just outside Sittingbourne. Many had to live under canvas in the grounds of the house. Each airwoman was issued with a ground sheet and six blankets. Hooks were fastened to the tent poles and uniforms were hung on these at night. In the morning the officers marched the girls back to Detling for their duties. This was the pattern for some considerable time after the raid, much to the displeasure of the WAAFs.

The men and women of 500 Squadron lost many of their possessions in the raid. Baths and fresh water became a luxury for a time at Detling. Frequent trips to Maidstone public baths were organised when it was realised that this was needed! Ever present was the threat of another raid before the present one was cleared and the possibility of invasion was still uppermost in people's minds. In the aftermath of the raid, the squadron still had to carry on with its operational duties. Richard Rogers remembers:

After the raid I found that of the few possessions I had, I had lost the better part in the bombing. Fortunately I was able to salvage a pocket-watch, my flying log-book and a few personal odds and ends which I had locked up in a suitcase. Of my uniform and clothing nothing much was left and, like many others, I had to be kitted out anew. I was flying on operations the next day, though there were a number of bomb-craters on the airfield which we had to negotiate during taxying, take-off and landing.

Squadron ground crews, helped by their aircrews, put in many extra hours of duty to repair the runways and to refuel and rearm the Ansons. One of the earliest aircraft to take off for a patrol after the raid was Anson 'Y', flown by Pilot Officer Peters. They very narrowly escaped when during the take-off the aircraft fell foul of a bomb crater. Only the skill of the pilot saved the crew from being killed and the aircraft being a write-off.

And so the blackest day in the history of the airfield came to an end. Familiar faces were missing in the messes, victims of the bombing and flying debris. Now the task of notifying the relatives of the dead and arranging for the burials had to be done.

A mass funeral was held at Maidstone cemetery for the majority of the dead. This was another harrowing experience for all those who attended and took part. The great yawning trench and the dozens of service lorries, and the seemingly unceasing chain of coffins. The funeral bearers, a number of them drawn from 500 Squadron, struggled and stumbled across the uneven grass. Large groups of weeping relatives and friends attended to pay their last respects to the dead. Many had travelled long distances and all through the night to be there. The station padre and several civilian clergy read the funeral service and finally the dead were buried in peace. Somehow, life at Detling would never be quite the same. A new aggressive attitude towards the enemy was beginning to show itself.

The funeral of the victims killed in the Detling air raid on 13 August 1940. Burial was at Sutton Road Cemetery. (*Kent Messenger*)

# 7

# From Detling To Bircham Newton

After being discharged from hospital in July/August 1940, after the incident of the ditching Anson at Dunkirk, Richard Rogers was given a fortnight's leave and pronounced medically fit for flying duties. He was also promoted to Sergeant! He remembers:

> I returned to the squadron on flying duties in early August and discovered that some of the aircraft in 'B' flight had been fitted with an enormous cannon. This weapon had a very long barrel and a bore which I believe was of 20 mm. The floor of the aircraft between the main spars in the cabin had been completely cut away and the cannon had been mounted at the point of balance on the rear spar with the barrel pointing downward and forward through the hole in the floor. It could not be swivelled from side to side but only in an up and down direction by either depressing or lifting the twin handles, one for each hand. The canisters containing the shells were very heavy and it was not easy to clip them when loaded on to the top of the breech.
>
> These cannon had been fitted for the purpose of attacking enemy 'E' boats which by now were a fairly common sight in the Channel constantly harrowing our ships. It was the wireless operator's job to load and fire this cannon, and very close co-operation with the pilot was necessary in order to achieve results.
>
> My first operation in August was in an aircraft so fitted. It was a night sortie when we were going out to 'gun' enemy shipping reported to be in the Straits of Dover. Unfortunately we were recalled after 20 minutes for some reason and diverted to Manston. Later on however, I did manage to fire the gun at enemy ships. When it was fired, the whole aircraft shook and reverberated, the cabin being filled with cordite fumes. I felt sometimes that the main spar would surely crack or that the remaining floor of the aircraft would splinter and we would all fall through. Once, when changing the bullet canister with the aircraft in a tight turn, I could not get it to engage properly in the breech. I jammed my gloved fingers in the mechanism and dropped the loaded canister. It went straight out of the hole in the floor and I saw it begin to roll over and over as it disappeared out of my line of vision towards the sea. Flying Officer

Armstrong, my pilot, later told me that he felt sure he saw it hit the fore-deck of an 'E' boat, but of this, none of us were certain.

With operations now back to normal after the dreadful raid of the 13th the squadron renewed its patrols with the new weapon fitted to the Ansons. The British Cannon Manufacturing Company had designed a special mounting for the aircraft to enable it to carry a cannon. It was presented to 500 Squadron in recognition of their success in escort duty and it was the first aircraft and first squadron in the world to fly with a free mounted cannon. When the cannon was fired rearwards the recoil added an extra five knots to the Anson's speed!

The next day, the 14th, the Air Officer Commanding-in-Chief, Air Vice Marshal Marix and Air Commodore Cowcan visited the station to inspect the damage. When the extent of the damage and the number of deaths and casualties were presented to them, both men were sickened. They had nothing but praise for the way the station was attempting to get back on to its feet and at the continuance of duties by the squadron and staff at Detling.

That same evening the squadron was given the extra and unusual task of flying over London after dusk to check on the black-out system. From the air it was perfectly easy for the crews to see just where a source of light was coming from, whether it be from industrial sites or family homes. Each crew had to write to the Air Ministry suggesting ways in which the black-out could be improved. Though this duty sometimes proved very monotonous for the crews, it was a welcome relief from the strains of protecting our convoys against enemy action.

500 Squadron supported two aircraft flights, 'A' and 'B'. Whilst neither of them ranked superior to the other, they seemingly enjoyed a friendly rivalry. The flights had separate dispersal areas but meals were taken on the main camp, lorries being used to run the men back and forth. 'A' flight were dispersed at the southern end of the airfield and 'B' were similarly dispersed at the northern end by a row of houses that were now being used as a 'Waafery'. It was a wonderful feat of one-upmanship when either flight was called upon to provide replacement aircraft for one gone un-serviceable from the other flight. Forays to the local inns and hostelries produced many tense moments when one flight intruded into the other flight's 'local'. The 'Black Horse' and the 'White Horse' at Bearsted plus the 'Cock Horse' at Detling were 'A' flight territory whilst the 'Wheatsheaf' and the 'Three Squirrels' belonged to 'B' flight. In between these was 'no-man's land'! Jack Hoskins recalls:

> I remember 'B' flight had a rather treasured monopoly set. One afternoon in August it was cunningly 'borrowed' by a member of 'A' flight, the ruffians flight! Crossing in front of an Anson running its engines up on the apron, it was promptly blown out of his hands by the slip-stream. Amid cards and paper money blowing everywhere, the culprit beat a hasty retreat leaving the monopoly set scattered to high heaven.

That same evening in the local pub, we were discussing the dastardly trick played on us. A civilian, overhearing the conversation promptly produced his wallet and insisted on giving us the money for a new set of monopoly. It was duly purchased amid great pomp and ceremony and left, wrapped up in a cloth in 'B' flight crew room.

When the Luftwaffe bombed us on the 13th the crew room was hit. When the 'all clear' sounded, two of us ran to retrieve our treasured monopoly set. We arrived just in time to see again the cards and paper money being blown into every bomb crater in sight. 'A' flight had the last laugh on us that time.

As the end of August approached, enemy activity around the area began to increase. Lone raiders and reconnaissance planes began to fly across the airfield. On 30 August, at 17.20 hours, Detling was subjected to another sizeable raid.

The radar and Observer Corps had plotted a big force of enemy aircraft making for the Coastal Command airfield at Eastchurch on the Isle of Sheppey. Just as it crossed the English coast, the force seemed to divide and the main fighter escort made for Detling.

With the sirens beginning to wail on the field, Captain Eschwege, the Luftwaffe escort commander leading 1/3G 52 swept low over the boundary at Detling, the Messerschmitt 109 and 110s firing cannon and machine guns. The 110s dropped high explosive and delayed action bombs. The fuel dumps were set on fire and the runway was badly straddled, putting it temporarily out of use. The main electricity cable to the airfield was cut leaving the base out of communication for 15 hours. The Operations Record Book stated:

30.8.40— Amplification of report of raid.
23.20 hrs— 40 to 50 bombs were dropped, size variable from 40 lb to 100 lb approx. Airfield rendered u/s.
Casualties—1 killed—1 injured. Identity not established. 1 aircraft destroyed. Airfield estimated repairable by 08.00 hrs 31.8.40.

Whilst only a few casualties resulted, the devastation was again intense. During the following night, whilst the clearance from the previous raid was still going on, Detling was attacked by several lone raiders. As they had mistakenly thought Detling to be a Fighter Command airfield, these attacks were a wasted effort for the Luftwaffe. In no way did it impair the ability of the Command to carry on fighting the Battle of Britain.

September and autumn seemed to arrive simultaneously. As a break from escorting the ships in convoy, attacks were made on German vessels. The barges, lying in the harbours and waiting for the invasion orders, were attacked. German-held strongholds were bombed and gunned. As if in retaliation, Detling received another attack on 2 September. The element of surprise was again achieved by the enemy, the cloud affording them good cover.

The attack was carried out at high level by a Gruppe of Dornier 17s. Flying high over the southern end of the airfield, they dropped about 100 high explosive bombs on the field, again causing great damage. Not one of the permanent buildings was hit but the taxi and runways were badly pitted. The airfield was rendered unserviceable for three hours. The Civil Defence sealed off all approach roads to Detling in case this was the long awaited prelude to invasion. No enemy forces materialised and the surrounding area was opened to traffic once again.

With the Battle of Britain now at its height, the squadron aircraft continued to fly out of Detling at low level heading straight towards the Channel. From the airfield it took about seventeen minutes to reach the coast-line. Now there was black oily smoke to be seen, either from a sinking ship or aircraft or the smoke from heavy guns. The usual exit point was Dover and now a sinister looking line of barrage balloons had sprung up. Whilst these were a deterrent to the enemy aircraft, the Ansons also approached them with due caution!

September turned out to be a very sunny and warm month. To the aircrews the Channel appeared so very calm, like a placid lake. This created the impression that the enemy coast was even nearer, and this in itself brought moments of danger, as Richard Rogers remembers:

> We carried on with our Channel patrols throughout September. On the 24th we took off at 10.55 in Anson N.5355, flown by Flying Officer Armstrong, for our usual search in the Straits. On that day I was detailed for both gunnery and wireless. Flying Officer Armstrong spotted a single-engined Henschel spotter plane about half-way across the Channel heading for the French coast. We went straight in to attack using the fixed Browning front gun in the nose. It was a decoy for immediately we were sprung upon by three 109 fighters diving down at us from out of the sun. We turned for home at sea level. I fired continually from the rear turret and had the satisfaction of seeing the leading fighter turn away after his attack with intermittent puffs of smoke issuing from under his engine. The other two pounded us pretty much as we fish-tailed and weaved about, but they broke off the attack when we crossed the Kent coast.
>
> I was called forward urgently by Flying Officer Armstrong and was very much taken aback when I saw the mess in the cabin. The wireless equipment was completely shattered and had I been sitting there, as usually I did, I would have been blown to pieces. There were a lot of holes in the fuselage, some broken windows and torn fabric. I went up beside Flying Officer Armstrong, who was looking very pale. He shouted in my ear that he had been hit in the legs and asked me to stay with him. There was blood from his wounds seeping through his flying clothing and some also on the floor near the rudder pedals. I will never know how he managed to pilot the aircraft, but I map-read for him and eventually we arrived back over Detling and fired off a succession of red verey cartridges.
>
> I saw the ambulance and fire-tender move out below and position themselves in readiness. We came in on a steady, fairly flat approach and landed in a slightly uphill

direction. Near the end of the landing run the aircraft turned into a gentle ground loop as Flying Officer Armstrong was unable to correct the swing due to his injuries. We quickly got him out and into the waiting ambulance which conveyed him straight into Rochester/Chatham hospital. It was a bad feeling to have death so near to you.

On 5 September, the Luftwaffe landed at Detling. It was not the prophesied invasion but more a case of being lost. The aircraft was a Messerschmitt 109 piloted by Oberleutnant Carl-Heinz Metz. Hearing the sound of an aircraft approaching, the watch at Detling sounded the siren. Looking to the north of the airfield, a single aircraft was seen to lower its undercarriage. The siren stopped and, to the amazement of all the duty personnel, an enemy aircraft did one circuit and landed. The fire tender and guard truck raced to intercept the 109 but the pilot brought the aircraft to a halt. Standing up in the cockpit, Carl-Heinz Metz raised his hands above his head and gracefully surrendered. The guards helped him from his aircraft and swiftly marched him off to the guard room and interrogation.

Some time after, it was stated that the pilot had realised he was hopelessly lost and short of fuel when he sighted the airfield just a few miles away. Rather than face a wet crash-landing in the Channel, he lowered his wheels and landed. Later he was transferred to a prison camp and the intact aircraft was flown to Farnborough for evaluation by the 'boffins'. It did prove however, that even fighter pilots had their navigational problems!

With the war now one year old, it became anyone's guess as to just how long it would last. It was evident that the Luftwaffe, for all its bombing of the fighter airfields, would not clear the Royal Air Force from the skies over England. Many thought it would all be over by Christmas, others felt the invasion would come earlier, and some were hesitant to voice an opinion. Something or someone did however influence the Luftwaffe for on 7 September the battle entered a new phase. Adolf Hitler called off the offensive against the sector airfields of Fighter Command and commenced the bombing of our cities. Whilst this was a welcome respite for the RAF, the might of the enemy was now directed against the civilian population.

With this change in German policy, a signal was received from the Air Ministry sending 'A' flight of 500 Squadron on detachment to Bircham Newton in Norfolk. This meant that eight aircraft would be deployed from Detling to this base in East Anglia. With Flight Sergeant Wilson in charge of the ground crews consisting of twelve engine fitters, twelve riggers, ten armourers, six wireless engineers, six electricians and ten ancillary tradesmen, the transport was loaded with kit and spares and the journey to the east coast began.

On arrival at Bircham, 'A' flight found it not dissimilar to Detling. The climate proved very cold and it was frequently foggy. The flight was billeted in the only available building left vacant—the First World War de-contamination block! It was really not fit for human habitation but the possibility of a gas attack during the opening stages of the present war had ensured the survival of the building. With a little dab of paint here and a piece of issue lino there, it had improved, but only in appearance. It still remained a most uncomfortable home for the detached flight.

The Ansons of 'A' operated day and night in a similar role to that which they had known at Detling, reconnaissance and anti-shipping strikes together with occasional leaflet drops. There was also the constant threat of enemy aircraft to contend with. John Thompson told me:

> When we were at Bircham I used to drive a lorry with about half of my dispersal crew down to lunch, the mess being quite a distance from our dispersal area. Lunch usually took about one hour and afterwards we would all congregate at the flight office ready to board and go back to our own area of the field.
>
> One particular day I was checking through the 700s (aircraft log-books) in the flight office whilst waiting for some of the men to come back from the mess. I went to the door of the office to see if the late-comers had arrived when something moving at the end of the airfield attracted my attention.
>
> Coming towards the flight office at about 100 feet above the ground was a Heinkel HE 111 K. It zoomed across the grass, firing its front guns and was rapidly coming in my direction. Being a hero, I froze instantly! I just could not believe it. Bullets were landing all around me and I could see that the bomb doors were open ready to drop the big one.
>
> All the lads had thrown themselves to the ground or taken refuge under the lorry. With a terrible roar, the aircraft swept over the flight office but no bomb was dropped. A minute later something fell away from the aircraft and with a terrific thud landed near the office. It was not the expected bomb but part of the actual bomb release gear. The army manning the bunkers and pill-boxes around the airfield were firing everything at the enemy plane. As quickly as it appeared, with a roar it had gone.
>
> Later on I heard that it had crashed at Fakenham near Cromer. Whatever had fallen off had caused the crash to take place and with the bombs still on board, not much remained of the crew or the aircraft. It was sheer luck that it did not drop them over the flight office or we should all have been killed. No air raid warning was given, I suppose there was not really time. It certainly gave us all a fright.

Whilst 'A' flight was having a tense time at Bircham Newton, the remainder of the squadron back at Detling were also having their problems.

November arrived bringing fog and low cloud to Detling. This weather severely hampered the activities of the squadron. This together with the fact that the Anson was rapidly becoming obsolete, meant that the crews had to be selective in what they were able to do. With German aircraft now ranged all along the French coast, it became obvious that the Anson was no match for the enemy aircraft. There was talk among the squadron that it would soon be getting a faster and more modern aircraft. Though they all regretted to see the faithful Anson go, many had longed for a change.

Meanwhile, the patrols had to be carried out. One most unfortunate incident, not connected with operational duties, happened on 8 November. Taking a well-earned break from active flying duty, Pilot Officer Chaffey and Pilot Officer Mallalieu decided to take the squadron Miles Magister communications plane to visit a friend who was serving at another airfield in the south-west. Taking off from a clear Detling in the morning, the Magister was flying over Ightham when it mysteriously crashed. Sadly both men lost their lives, and the squadron lost two very good pilots.

December proved to be a fairly quiet month, many operations being cancelled due to the bad weather. There were limited hours of daylight and the fog, rain and snow seemed fairly persistent. The weather hampered friend and foe alike. This gave the station a chance to make good much of the damage caused by the bombing. New sleeping quarters and mess halls were being built both by civilian builders and by the Ministry of Works and Buildings Department. The 'civvies', who were obviously on peace work and therefore eager to put in many more working hours, seemed to leave the ministry 'types' behind when it came to speed of building. This naturally caused some friction between the two groups, even to the extent of the ministry men demanding equal rights of pay and stating they were prepared to 'down tools' in protest. After hurriedly arranged talks, the matter was resolved and building at Detling began at a far faster pace.

Christmas was celebrated in traditional style, the officers serving the airmen their dinner before retiring to their own mess. The bars stayed open all day and many lived to regret it! It was hoped to mount some flying operations on Christmas Day but dull weather and low cloud made sure that the squadron stayed on the ground. The last entry in the squadron's Operations Record Book stated thus:

31.12.40— Details of Operational Flying—500 Squadron.
No. of convoys escorted—31.
 No. of reconnaissances—272.
 Aerial combats—5. Action against enemy subs—nil, but 6 MTBs bombed.
Total No. of flying hours—1,386 52 mins.
Average No. of aircraft available—13.
No. of crews—12.

So ended 1940. Just what 1941 would bring to 500 Squadron was anyone's guess.

An Anson of 500 Squadron over Kent.

Daphne Pearson pictured at Hendon some time after receiving her George Cross. (*Daphne Pearson*)

Daphne Pearson (now section officer) and her George Cross. (*IWM*)

# 8

# Ansons To Blenheims

The New Year opened with the *London Gazette* announcing that ten members of the squadron had received mentions in despatches. Tragically three of them had been killed before they knew of their awards.

Daphne Pearson had been promoted to assistant section officer towards the end of 1940 and had also been to Buckingham Palace to collect her medal. On a hot day she had attended the investiture by the King at the Palace. She was presented with the medal that ranks next to the Victoria Cross, the medal of the Military Division of the British Empire Medal for Gallantry—the EGM. Daphne, in her very unassuming nature, said that it was a very hot day. Nearly all the men attending fainted and the women spent most of their time fetching water for the them!

With the Battle of Britain resulting in a victory for Fighter Command, life at Detling had taken a more stabilised turn. Building was still going on, repairing much of the damage done by the Luftwaffe raids. Damage of this type was easily repairable but not so the damage done to the morale of the men and women of the squadron. This was only to be expected with the idle frustration of staying on the ground because of the bad weather plus the bad living conditions since the previous year's raids. This combined with the ageing Anson pushed morale in the squadron a little low.

January and February were dreadful flying months, there was little doing in the air. When the weather did allow, the squadron carried on with the usual duties of convoy escort and mine spotting.

In March, Wing Commander Turner left the squadron and 'A' flight returned from Bircham Newton, glad to be back within the fold of 500 Squadron. Wing Commander Turner had seen 500 through a most difficult period of its existence. Much of the grief of death he had felt personally for the men and women who had died under his command.

Wing Commander M. Q. Candler was posted to the squadron as Commanding Officer and it was during his time of command that the rumours of new aircraft for the squadron became fact.

At midnight on 7 April 1941, the squadron temporarily ceased operations with the versatile but obsolete Anson. Many of the squadron were sad to see the old Anson go, but they all knew that the squadron could progress no further without a newer aircraft.

On 8 April, they began to convert to the Bristol Blenheim Mk IV. Powered by two 840 hp Bristol Mercury engines, the Blenheim was a light bomber so small as to be cramped, but still unlike anything the Royal Air Force had previously possessed. Under the mid-wing was a small bay for a bomb load of 1,000 lb. A single .303 Lewis or Vickers gun was mounted in a prominent dorsal turret and a single Browning of the same calibre was fixed in the left wing. With a cruising speed of 200 mph it was pleasant to fly and highly manoeuvrable. With a speed much in excess of the Anson, it also supported armour and self-sealing tanks. Conversion to the type began immediately.

The crews of 500 took to the new aircraft very quickly. Sharing Detling with 48 squadron, who already flew the type, was a help in the conversion period from Ansons to Blenheims. Within a matter of weeks they had settled into an operational routine.

April passed into May and the rumours of a move to another station began. Sure enough on 15 May, orders were received to this effect:

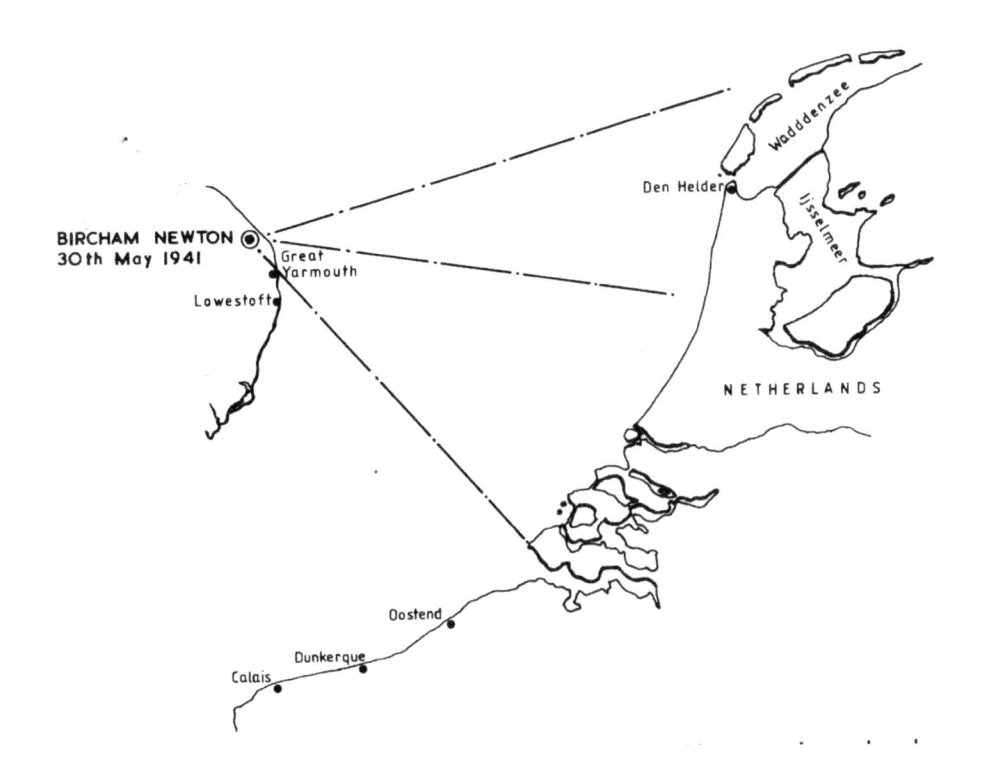

'I say, the news is that 500 are on the move.'
'Really, how can they bear to leave Detling.'
'Dunno but they are.'
'Where to?'
'Rumours are Norfolk somewhere!'

The aircraft left Detling on the morning of 16 May 1941 to fly to Bircham Newton on the east coast. The base was familiar to 'A' flight, in fact it had not really changed since their detachment there. The ground crews and transport, together with kit and all the necessities of a squadron, arrived sometime later.

For nearly three years Detling had been home to 500 Squadron. It had shared in their joy and their sorrow. It had seen their triumphs and their despairs. Now, with newer aircraft and a new airfield to fly from, the squadron looked forward to more success than they had been used to.

500 now accepted responsibility for the North Sea convoys stretching from Yorkshire, down the east coast to the Thames Estuary. With this familiar role came a new one, that of search and rescue sorties for fighter and bomber aircrew who had ditched in the treacherous North Sea. A few days after the squadron had arrived at Bircham Newton, one such operation took place and brought 500 back into contact with the Luftwaffe.

Blenheim 'T' Tommy was scrambled for an air sea rescue mission on 30 May. Sighting the downed airmen in the water, a dinghy was dropped from the Blenheim. As the aircraft turned for another pass over the unfortunate pilot in the sea, three

500 squadron Bristol Blenheim, Bircham Newton Nov 40-May 42. (*J. Wilson*)

yellow-nosed 109s came out of the cloud firing cannon and machine guns. Whirling and weaving to get out of the way of the enemy, the Blenheim's turret gunner took his opportunity and sent his bullets pounding into one of the 109s. Seeing smoke pouring from his engine, the 109 turned for France, the other two following with some haste. This marked the squadron's first contact with the enemy since arriving at their new home.

The North Sea also provided sanctuary for the German convoys. Hugging the Dutch coast, they would travel from Denmark and Norway to the German held ports in France and beyond. They also provided targets for the bombs of the Blenheims. Amongst the various successes scored by the squadron was a Swedish cargo boat of 6,123 tons. The boat had been chartered by the Germans for carrying iron ore. This received the attention of the squadron and was finally sunk off Borkum.

High summer came and the North Sea began to warm up, both in water temperature and combat. The long summer evenings gave valuable extra hours for flying and for carrying the war back into Europe. The need for blackout, even on summer evenings did however create its problems for the aircrew. John Thompson remembers:

> The gun pits and pill boxes around the airfield at Bircham Newton were manned by men of the Welsh Regiment. They were there to protect the field in the case of a paratroop attack and to defend the aircraft standing out at dispersal areas. The runway was lit by flares only on the odd occasion in case the enemy should spot it from the air. Hence most of the flying, even during the darkest of nights, was a risky business when taking off or landing.
>
> One particular night a Blenheim of one of the other squadrons started down the darkened runway in preparation to take off. As it reached about half-way, there was a blinding flash and it crashed right beside one of the pill boxes. We thought it had been shot down by enemy aircraft but later found out that it had come off the runway. The pilot received a broken back in the crash and was unable to leave the aircraft which by now was burning badly.
>
> A gunner in the nearby pill box jumped down from his position and ran to the burning aircraft, dragging the pilot out and away from the wreck. Whilst we all thought that the man deserved a medal for his courage, he was in fact put on a charge for leaving his own post whilst on duty. So much for justice!

With the lack of hangars at Bircham Newton, the Blenheims of 500 had to remain outside. The fitters put forward the idea of engine tents. These were intended to protect the engines from frost and rain. They were inflatable and were so designed as to fit snugly around the engine. When not in use, the instructions stated that they must be deflated upon removal. This obviously proved rather a chore and one bright ground crew man devised a new and easier method. John Thompson again:

To save the trouble of having to blow them up each evening, and against all the rules, the engine tents were lifted off intact in the morning and placed over the side of the fence that ran along the side of our dispersal. This way they also served as a very dry place in which to sit during the rain. This was used to the extent of even putting a stove inside them!

One rather blustery day, Ken Springett was running up the engines of a Blenheim on the hard apron. Peering out of his front window, to his horror he saw one of the engine tents being blown along, straight towards the turning propellers. Looking like a pendulous 'Michelin' man it approached Ken at furious pace. Quickly switching off the engine ignition, he saw the tent wrap itself around the port propeller. It ripped like a disembowelled rabbit and was sucked up into the engine.

Jumping down from the aircraft, he tried to pull the tent away from the engine but without success. It finally took several of the ground crew and quite a few hours to remove it completely. Needless to say, several heads rolled over the incident, charges were issued and all future removals were deflated properly.

In July, command of the squadron was given to Wing Commander G.T. Gilbert. Wing Commander Candler, having seen the squadron settled into their new station, was posted to another squadron.

With the new commander came a signal that was to send 'A' flight on yet another detachment, this time to Harrowbeer just outside Plymouth. This was one of the airfields that had been opened recently.

The flight was based there for the new role of attacking the U-boat pens at St Nazaire and the dockyard installations lying alongside. Though this detachment was only of short duration, the flight received many successes for the loss of only two aircraft.

At Bircham Newton it was business as usual. News reached them that Daphne Pearson had again been to Buckingham Palace to exchange her Gallantry Medal for the George Cross. Though she had now left the squadron, she kept contact with many friends in the squadron.

On 24 August, Blenheim 'Q' for Queenie set out on a routine search and rescue patrol over the North Sea. The crew, Pilot Officer Fletcher, Sergeant Mylieu and Sergeant Walton were very experienced members of the squadron. The weather was clear with fleecy cloud at about 3,000 feet. It was perfect flying weather. Contact with the aircraft was lost as the sortie was just ending and the aircraft did not return to Bircham Newton. It was assumed that the aircraft crashed into the sea. Another search was instigated but no wreckage or life rafts were found.

Under similar circumstances, Blenheims 'B' and 'V' did not return from patrol on 30 August. Again the weather was clear and the loss remained unexplained. In September 1941, permission was given by the Ministry for the squadron to commence 'Intruder' missions over enemy airfields. This new role alternated with the sorties to attack enemy shipping. With more aircraft now available, the squadron Blenheims were often escorted by Spitfires thus ensuring their full concentration on the bombing and leaving the enemy fighters to the Spitfires. On 31 October a 10,000 ton merchant ship was set on fire, sadly with the losses of Squadron Leader Phipps and Sergeant Mowan and their crews. Another Blenheim that took part in the attack, Z.6161, piloted by Squadron Leader Wilf Butler returned safely to base. On landing, Wilf Butler understood that the ship had been completely destroyed. He also understood that the air officer commanding 16 group had recommended him for an immediate DFC for his part in the attack. However no such decoration came his way and it was assumed that it had misfired in the channels of recommendation and approval. There were other times when an award was thought to be deserved, especially when members of 500 Squadron were recruited to work on behalf of the Army. John Thompson told me of one task he was given:

Sometimes we had to take on the job of identifying wreckage or remains of crashed aircraft for the army intelligence. One such incident concerned a crashed Blenheim of the squadron that shared Bircham Newton with us. Unfortunately it had crashed into the sea just off the coast at Cromer and the wreckage was washed ashore some days later.

The east coast at this time was heavily mined in case of invasion. On this particular occasion I was detailed to look at the remains of the crash and for this purpose a very officious army officer was detailed to brief me on the operation. We arrived at the spot where the pieces were beached just above the water line. The officer stated that if I followed the tape to and across the beach, I would come to no harm and would not step on any of the mines buried in the shingle and sand.

I gingerly made my way across the beach, treading as though I were treading on pingpong balls! With my tongue in my cheek and my heart thumping, the distance to the wreckage seemed as though it stretched for miles. Eventually I reached it without mishap and began to sift through the pieces of aircraft. After about ten minutes I found a piece of engine casing with a serial number on it. I related the numbers to the army officer who immediately murmured 'Oh God' to himself. Mentioning the same phrase to himself several times more, I realised that the serial number was familiar to the officer and that this wreckage was indeed the aircraft that he had assumed it to be. Returning to the mainland, I noticed that the man had a very worried look about him and I pondered on this afterwards. Maybe the aircraft carried someone or something very important to the war effort. It was apparent that the loss of the aircraft was a great loss to the military authorities. For myself, it was just another job carried out in extremely dangerous and nerve-racking circumstances. I never again wanted to walk a minefield!

'A' flight returned from Harrowbeer to the good news that the squadron was again to convert to a new and more powerful aircraft, the Lockheed Hudson. Of

American origin, it was the first American-built aircraft to see operational service in Coastal Command. With a crew of five, it was powered by two Wright-Cyclone engines, later to be superseded by Pratt and Whitney twin wasp engines. The armament was superior to the Blenheim with fixed twin .303 forward guns, twin .303 guns in a dorsal turret and one .303 in a ventral position. With a maximum speed of 246 mph it had a flying endurance of six hours. Historians have said that the era of the Hudsons was the finest phase in the squadron's history.

By the end of November, 500 had fully converted to the new aircraft and were back carrying out anti-shipping and convoy duties combined with bombing enemy held harbours. With the approach of Christmas, the weather began to hamper operations. Bircham Newton, in a very flat part of Norfolk, suffered badly from the gales that came in from the North Sea. Often visibility was down to a few hundred yards and the cloud base was oppressively low. Though this type of weather did not actually ground the squadron with their new aircraft, it did not help them achieve success either.

Christmas was met in the customary style of the officers serving the men Christmas lunch before retiring to their own mess. A few operations were mounted but nothing of significance. Each mess held its own party and for a time most thoughts of war were put aside. When the alcohol and food had taken effect and the air was filled by sounds of revelry, some found it a good time to meditate on the second Christmas of the war. Many had thought that it would have been over by now but whilst the enemy had not won the victory over the Royal Air Force in the sky, it was still very powerful and seemed to be gathering strength in certain quarters. Many could see the war lasting for the next year and beyond. However long it should last, one thing was uppermost in many of the minds of the personnel that made up 500 Squadron. They and the country would achieve victory in the end.

# 9
# U-boat Days

The New Year was heralded by another change in command for the squadron. Wing Commander Denis Spotswood arrived to take his position as commanding officer. This officer was no stranger to the Hudson, in the years previous he had been ferrying them across the Atlantic to take their place in the Air Force squadrons. From these humble beginnings, Wing Commander Spotswood rose to the rank of Air Chief Marshal and eventually became the Chief of the Air Staff. This was for the future but for the moment the new commanding officer was warmly welcomed to 500 Squadron.

1942 continued in similar fashion as the latter days of the past year. The search and rescue facility became more used as many of our fighter and bomber pilots were forced to ditch in the North Sea. At this time of the year the bitter cold of the sea was a great danger. A ditched pilot without a life-raft could not expect to last above ten minutes in the freezing conditions. Speed was therefore essential but not every sortie ended in success as the Operations Book faithfully recorded:

15.1.42—   Hudson 'A' ordered on search and rescue mission.
Crew:-P/O Grummer, F/S Oldfield, Sgt Ormer, Sgt Morgan.
Time up: 08.45. Time down: 12.15 hrs. Carried out search but did not sight dinghy. Sea moderate to rough.

On 30 January, one Hudson pilot showed great courage and flying skill. Pilot Officer M. A. Ensor, a relatively new officer to the squadron, carried out an attack on an enemy ship off Sylt, Germany. Hits were seen to register on the ship by the aircraft crew, when the shore batteries, aided by searchlights illuminating the aircraft, commenced a devastating attack on the Hudson. Diving for a lower altitude, Pilot Officer Ensor noticed that the altimeter still read 200 feet and assumed that he could go lower. To his horror he suddenly saw the sea rise up to meet him. Pulling back rapidly on the control column, to his further dismay his instruments told him that the starboard engine had failed and that the electrical system was faulty.

Receiving a course for home from the navigator, Pilot Officer Ensor headed across the North Sea on one engine. After five and a half hours, with his fuel tanks virtually dry, he assumed he was over English soil. Realising that he would not make Bircham Newton, he fired the recognition flares of the day and seeing a large field ahead, prepared to belly land his aircraft.

Just over the boundary hedge Pilot Officer Ensor dropped the Hudson on the soft grass and gradually slid to a standstill. Remarkably, not one of the crew sustained a scratch and the aircraft was not a total loss.

In March, 'B' flight were sent on detachment to Limavady in Northern Ireland. Here they were engaged in the task of helping to combat the U-boat menace in the Atlantic shipping lanes. The German submarines had adopted the tactics of hunting and sinking shipping in large 'wolf' packs, several or more submarines taking part in a single operation.

Whilst this detachment took place, the rest of the squadron left Bircham Newton and moved to Stornaway in the Outer Hebrides. It was to many far colder and bleaker than Bircham. The accommodation was tented and the mess and dining hall was a large marquee. Some of the newer postings to the squadron wondered just what wrong they had done in their life to deserve such a rotten posting!

Back at Limavady, 'B' flight were pressing home their attacks with great enthusiasm. Although the submarines were heavily armed when they met them on the surface the aircrews carried on their relentless attacks. Hudsons 'A' and 'Q' claimed great success in April when two U-boats were left with their bows in the air. Carrying out the attack from low level, both crews flew through a barrage of fire to deliver their bomb load. They were both very accurate and the German craft were badly holed.

One attack especially earned Mike Ensor a DFC. A U-boat on the surface was sighted during one routine patrol. Wheeling the aircraft round, he dived at the submarine from a height of about 3,000 feet. He dropped all four Torpex charges simultaneously, and two of them straddled the enemy craft, blowing off the bow section. The last memory Mike Ensor had of the attack was seeing the majority of the U-boat crew scrambling to launch life-boats.

'B' flight now returned to join the rest of the squadron at Stornaway. The reunion at this very bleak base was not to be for long for orders were received to take the squadron to St Eval in Cornwall. This was not before Flight Lieutenant C. J. Mackenzie got the DFC and Flight Sergeants McCourt and Andrews, Mentions in Despatches for the many successful patrols they carried out from Stornaway.

In August the squadron arrived at the very homely airfield of St Eval. By comparison with Stornaway, it was a paradise. Less than 24 hours after their arrival, and before the main bulk of the squadron had arrived, the first operation was flown from this airfield. Flying Officer Blakely and his crew in Hudson 'A' dropped leaflets on French fishing vessels in the Bay of Biscay.

The Hudsons were proving a very reliable aircraft for 500. It was a sturdy and powerful machine creating more success for the squadron than they had previously known. It was ideal for the long hours of patrol that was the duty of the reconnaissance squadrons.

Operations continued at full pace throughout the lovely summer of 1942. The long warm days were a welcome relief from the past winter. Somehow life seemed a little better with the sun continually shining, the cool evenings just made for walking the lovely turf of Cornwall. The pleasure however was short-lived, new orders were received from the Air Ministry that were to make a dramatic change of life for 500 Squadron.

On the last day of August the squadron was ordered to cease operations in preparation for going overseas. The aircrew and aircraft flew to Gosport in Hampshire, the ground crew being posted to No. 2 PDC at Wilmslow in Cheshire for what was termed as 'strenuous training'.

Now the squadron was into the rigours of reorganising the manpower and arranging postings in and out of the squadron. The strength of the unit had to be increased for this new posting and the aircraft had to be fitted with long range tanks and other necessary modifications for the journey overseas.

As the structure of the squadron was changing, more decorations came through including a bar to the DFC for Flying Officer Ensor. Of the various parties held to celebrate the awards, one said goodbye to the women of the squadron. The WAAFs

500 Squadron Hudson attacking a German submarine in the Mediterranean, 1943. (*B. Lee*)

were not allowed overseas postings at this time. Having given stirling service in support of 500, it was only fitting that friends should part on such a note.

In October the Hudsons flew down to Portreath in Cornwall for the original camouflage to be covered in white paint to suit the environment in which they would be carrying out operations.

On 5 November, 500 Squadron said goodbye to England for some years, as nine white-painted Hudsons flew from Portreath to Gibraltar. The nine aircraft serialised K, D, J, U, B, L, P, Y and S arrived safely on the rock. The ground crew had travelled over and had arrived some days earlier, ensuring that everything was ready for the arrival of the aircraft. Thus the commencement of operations got away to a quick start. The next day, 7 November 1942, five aircraft were scrambled to carry out an anti-submarine patrol, as the Operation Records Book states:

> 7.11.42—5 Hudsons carried out anti-submarine sweep from base. 'Q' carried out aircraft protection of the MV 'Thomas Stone' which had been torpedoed 40 miles off Cape Polos. 'C' escorted a large convoy east of Gib as instructed. 4 Hudsons carried out a parallel sweep eastwards from base. 'U' sighted a U-boat conning tower 4 miles away and attacked with 4 depth charges which straddled the U-boats track as it was diving. After the attack the a/c circled and the U-boat resurfaced. The a/c then dived and released one 100 lb anti-submarine bomb to the port quarter. The bomb fell 10 ft short of the target and exploded. The U-boat then slipped back into the water leaving its bows exposed at an angle of 60 degrees for 4 minutes, and then disappeared. Bubbles appeared which were followed by large quantities of black oil which continued until the a/c left that area. 'J' observed a U-boat travelling fast on the surface 10 miles S of the fleet. A/c immediately attacked with depth charges straddling the U-boat whilst it was still on the surface. Large quantities of oil were observed and part of the U-boat disappeared beneath the sea. The sub was confirmed destroyed by a destroyer on escort duty. 'D' sighted a U-boat on the surface and dived to attack crossing over the boat as it started to dive. Depth charges hung up so the a/c made a ½ turn and released the 4 depth charges 3 secs after the U-boat had submerged, 50 yds ahead of the swirl. 3 mins later a streak of black bubbles appeared and these continued for 10 mins. Nothing further was seen although the a/c returned after 30 mins and searched along the U-boats track.

Confirmation of the sinking by Hudson 'U' came later when on 14 November, survivors were landed stating that they were from a U-boat that had been attacked and sunk by a white Hudson with the letter 'U' on the side.

The squadron was at last really getting the feel of the enemy and were enjoying more success than previously. As proof of this, three more U-boats had been attacked on 10th November, with one confirmed as sunk.

On 12th November, the allied landings at Oran in Algeria commenced. Twelve aircraft from 500 were detailed to cover the operation from the air. The enemy sent a variety of aircraft into battle yet only one Hudson was attacked. 'A' was caught by a Junkers 88 and a Heinkel 111 but received only minor damage. At the same time Hudson 'J', resplendent in French colours, flew General Giraud, his son, his aide and a secretary to Oran and then on to Blida, which was at this time manned by the French.

The General had escaped from Germany and as a gesture to his bravery, the Air Ministry insisted that he kept the aircraft for his personal use. General Giraud however returned it, with grateful thanks, saying that it was of far more use in 500 Squadron to help combat the U-boat menace.

After the landings the squadron moved to Tafaroui near Oran. As if to celebrate the move, Hudson 'G' shot down a Junkers 52 transport aircraft and on 15 November more success came when Squadron Leader Ian Patterson forced a U-boat to beach, with another one surrendering. The crew of the latter boat waved white towels as a sign of surrender whilst they waited for a ship to take them prisoner.

Unfortunately many personnel of the squadron found themselves in a similar predicament on the 16th. Much of the equipment and men were travelling to Tafaroui on the RMS *Strathallan*, a troop-ship of some considerable size. During the voyage she became the victim of enemy action and was set on fire just off Oran. The fire seemed to take hold very quickly, spreading from the centre where the hit was received, to the bows of the ship in minutes. So intense was the smoke that accompanied the flames that the commodore, for this was his flagship, ordered the men to abandon ship. By this time several others in the convoy had taken up position close by. Several hundred men jumped into the sea and were immediately rescued by these other ships. Some lives were lost and the experience remained a nightmare for a long time after.

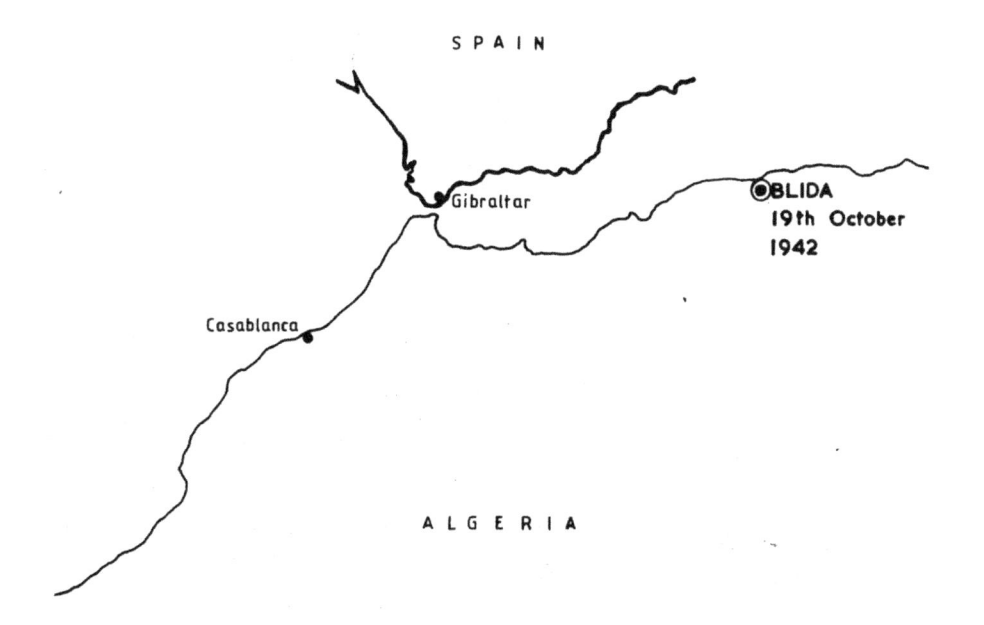

Success followed success at Tafaroui. Flying Officer Ensor again made a notable achievement, unfortunately with the loss of two of his crew. On a routine patrol, he was flying Hudson 'S' when he spotted a U-boat on the surface. He dived from 7,000 feet to just 50 feet. The U-boat saw him and began to submerge, but it was too late. Flying Officer Ensor's depth charges landed a direct hit on the craft's magazine or torpedoes. With a tremendous explosion the conning tower was ripped away and the sea rushed into the open wound.

So large was the explosion that the Hudson was badly hit by flying debris from the U-boat. Leaving the submarine fatally wounded, Flying Officer Ensor turned and made for Tafaroui. Approaching Algiers Bay, the port engine cut. Realising that he would have to ditch the Hudson in the sea, he ordered the crew to bale out. For some inexplicable reason, two of the members perished in the sea. Flying Officer Ensor and Sergeant Roe, the rear gunner, landed safely and were picked up by a sloop. Not realising at the time that the other members of the crew had perished, Ensor felt only sadness at the loss of his beloved aircraft as he watched 'S' for sugar sink slowly beneath the waves. A Distinguished Service Order was awarded him in recognition of his fine work with 500 Squadron. Now he was to be posted back to England to take up a staff post in Coastal Command Headquarters at Northwood in Middlesex.

The commanding officer, Wing Commander Spotswood, himself flew on many operations in the squadron. In company with Flying Officer H. M. S. Green, he dived his Hudson on to a U-boat just as it was submerging. The depth charges opened up the seams of the enemy craft and it came back to the surface with the crew firing sub-machine guns at the Hudson. This duel lasted for almost an hour until the U-boat sank close to the shore. The survivors waded inland and were taken prisoner by waiting French troops. For this operation, Wing Commander Spotswood was awarded the DFC.

Other aircraft were also successful in operations. Hudson 'Z' attacked a U-boat which immediately surrendered. Keeping watch over it, the pilot of the Hudson directed the U-boat commander to make for the nearest allied port. Within hours of reaching port, a Fleet Air Arm Albacore flying from HMS *Formidable* saw the U-boat and not noticing the white flag flying from the conning tower, dropped its torpedo. His aim was true and with a tremendous explosion the U-boat sank. Robbed of their prize, the crew of 'Z' felt very cheated and immediately upon landing sent a very strong letter of complaint to the Admiralty. Nothing however evolved from the letter and it was put down to the hazards of war.

On 19 November the squadron left Tafaroui for Blida near Algiers. Similar in size to their last base, their first impressions did not do much for the morale and well-being of the squadron.

When they arrived at Blida, the camp was found to have proper barrack blocks, something of a luxury for 500. The base was originally occupied by the French Air Force and contained both proper toilet facilities and very good permanent

RMS *Strathallan* abandoned and on fired off Oran, carrying personnel of 500 squadron. (*B. Lee*)

Tafaroui, 9 November 1942, Hudson being refuelled by an Arab chain gang. (*J. Wilson*)

buildings. All of this was fine to tired eyes until the barrack blocks were opened to allow the men to find themselves each a bed. The blocks were found to be alive with vermin, bugs of all sizes ran across the bunks, floors and ceilings. The medical officer ordered all the beds to be burnt and together with his team of orderlies began the job of disinfecting the blocks. Each airman was issued with three blankets, a pillow and a straw-filled mattress.

The end of November arrived with the record of 201 sorties having been flown in the 24 days of operations. The Royal Navy had confirmed that five U-boats had been sunk and many probables. The squadron had never known such success.

In December Hudson 'W' shot down the Cant 1007 bomber reconnaissance aircraft that was escorting an Italian submarine, afterwards managing to sink the submarine as well. One week later the same aircraft became the victim of a flying accident and was lost. The next day Hudson 'M' came to grief after destroying a submarine. The crew however were rescued by a Walrus aircraft of the local air-sea rescue detachment and were back on operations within hours.

And so the fourth Christmas of the war arrived. This year however it was different from the others. Flight Lieutenant Holmes flew out from the UK in a Hudson Mk III bringing mail for all ranks of the squadron. Christmas greetings and parcels were in great abundance from the loved ones left behind in the UK. Unfortunately due to the assassination of Admiral Darlan on Christmas Eve, Blida and Algiers were out of bounds to all personnel. The traditional Christmas did however take place, organised by the competent hands of Flight Lieutenant Paine DFM. Though a long way from home, it seemed as though a hand had only to be stretched out-to bring it all closer.

Hudsons at Tafaroui, 9 November 1942, and various American aircraft. (*J. Wilson*)

Crashed Hudson of 500 Squadron Tafaroui, 1943. (*B. Lee*)

'F' Freddie at Blida, 1942–43, Hudson aircraft. (*J. Wilson*)

# 10

# Overseas

The New Year was celebrated by the squadron being honoured with more awards. The DFC was announced for Squadron Leader Ian Patterson, Flight Lieutenants A. W. Barwood, J. B. Ensor, A. Holmes and Pilot Officer Criswell and the DFM for Sergeant H. J. Roe.

The New Year also bought the newer Mk V and VI Hudson to the squadron. This variant differed from the Mk I that the crews were at present flying in that the engines were now Pratt and Whitney twin Wasps. This gave the aircraft a higher speed and longer range. Newly trained crews now joined the squadron and a very intensive training campaign commenced in January to bring the new aircraft and the crews up to operational standard.

The U-boat menace was still present, seemingly in ever increasing force. The airborne radar that the new aircraft carried helped in finding the enemy. When the troop-ship *Windsor Castle* was torpedoed, it was Hudson 'D' that found the submarine and destroyed it as it attempted to dive.

One of the problems of operating in North Africa was the hot and fierce wind that blew unceasingly. Known as the Sirocco, it attempted but failed to halt the squadron's operations. This fact bought a response from General Spaatz who was commanding the North West African Air Forces at this time. In the form of a letter he sent thanks to Wing Commander Spotswood for providing air cover and ensuring a safe landing of American troops in North Africa.

So the routine of anti-submarine strikes continued for the squadron. So far 1943 had seen the destruction of many German U-boats and on 23 April came a most unusual happening.

Hudson 'N' was on routine patrol when the air-borne radar operator Flight Sergeant Kempster picked up a surface contact about twelve miles ahead of the aircraft. Increasing speed, the crew came upon a U-boat recharging its batteries on the surface. Turning into attack the enemy, the bomb doors on the Hudson opened ready to drop the charges. At this precise moment, the U-boats gun scored a direct hit on the Hudson killing the pilot instantly.

With the aircraft rapidly diving to the sea, Flight Sergeant Kempster took over the controls and brought it level as the other members of the crew removed the pilot from his seat. Sergeant Blackwell meanwhile had instantly closed the bomb doors lest further hits from the U-boats gun exploded the charges in the belly of the Hudson.

As the aircraft turned back over the U-boat, the gunner Sergeant Carruthers fired 600 rounds into it as a last protest. This sent the enemy crew scattering but did little damage to the submarine. The problem now was to fly the damaged Hudson back to Blida.

Sergeant Blackwell managed to keep the aircraft flying. Within sight of their base, the crew realised that the undercarriage had been shot away and that a landing was impossible. Taking the aircraft up to 500 feet, the rest of the crew managed to bale out safely including Sergeant Blackwell. Though the aircraft crashed into the sea and was lost, valuable aircrew were saved. Two weeks later came the news that Sergeant Blackwell had been awarded the Conspicuous Gallantry Medal and Flight Sergeant Kempster the DFM.

With the advent of April came a change of command for 500 Squadron. Wing Commander Spotswood who had led the squadron so very well, left to join the Directorate of Air Tactics. His successor was Wing Commander D. G. Keddie.

As the Wing Commander arrived to take up his posting, No. 614 (County of Glamorgan) squadron arrived at Blida with their Blenheim 'V' aircraft. 500

Hudson Q of 'B' Flight, Blida 1943. (*J. Wilson*)

being the older residents at Blida, were instructed to 'parent' the new squadron. It proved a good relationship and together with 608 (North Riding) squadron, the three squadrons added many more kills to their tallies. This was helped by the introduction of rocket projectiles for the Hudsons of 500. Geoffrey Cardew remembers working with them:

> I was posted from a maintenance unit in Algiers in late August, early September 1943 to 500 Squadron. I was a corporal armourer/fitter and was set to work on Hudsons in the maintenance flight. I had worked on the aircraft in 1942 when I was attached to 279 squadron at Bircham Newton and except for the new and highly secret rockets, four under each wing, I was therefore quite familiar with the work. The squadron was engaged on anti-submarine patrols and the aircraft carried 250 lb depth charges as well as rockets, forward firing Browning machine guns and Boulton and Paul turrets.
>
> Just before I arrived, the flight stationed at Tafaroui had by mistake let off a rocket from one of the Hudsons. One of the armourers testing the circuitry had left a plug in one of the rockets and misguidedly, the electrician in the cockpit had switched on the master switch. Whoosh! Away went the rocket with a flash and a roar, into a railway embankment some way away, straight through it and then made a 25' crater on the other side. The unfortunate electrician, as well as a court-martial, had literally wet himself with fright!

These rockets greatly enhanced the strike capability of the squadron and the crews learnt to fire them with far more accuracy than just dropping depth-charges on the U-boats.

As autumn approached in Blida, something reminiscent of Detling days came to many of the personnel of the squadron. This was 'drama'. Geoffrey Cardew again:

> The highlight of the autumn months was a cabaret show we put on entitled 'Café Coastal'. It was produced by Max Taylor, an enthusiastic amateur who persuaded, cajoled and bullied his cast into doing the impossible. There was 'Loonie Tune' Wallis, who provided the music, Max Taylor as the 'Wicked Squire' and myself as 'True Blue Harold' who saved the heroine from the dastardly villain. Scenery and props were gathered and scrounged from all over the place. Any piece of rubbish that was not wanted for any specific purpose was put to good use for the sake of the 'production'. I really cannot remember much about the response from our audience but it must have been quite good because not long after we put on our most ambitious effort of the entire war.
>
> The show was 'Cinderella' set in the future year of 6943. It seemed to take priority above all else. I cannot recall much of the actual work that we did on the airfield at this time. Servicing the aircraft, checking turrets and ammunition, cleaning and so on are just a blur on the memory, yet I remember very vividly the rehearsals which seemed to go on all day and night. The flurry of scenery construction and the painting of the

Air crews at Blida, North Africa. C/O was Wing Commander Spotswood, 1943. (*G. Cardew*)

*Above left:* Rocket practice on a smoke-filled float, 1943. (*J. Thompson*)

*Above right:* Flight sergeant J. C. Thompson, Blida, 1943. (*J. Thompson*)

'Cinderella 6943', La Senia 1943-44. (*G. Cardew*)

props seemed never ending. Other airmen were busy making all sorts of costumes out of bits and pieces scrounged from heaven knows where. I had a Nazi tank flag, picked up on a battlefield just outside Tunis, but this unfortunately was vandalized for the sake of the show and finished up as one of the 'gremlin's' wings!

The theatre was a large store house packed with hard biscuits, British, in 10 lb tins like petrol cans. Across these tins we laid planks of wood for benches. During many of the shows, the audience would plunge their hands beneath the seats and come up with a handful of biscuits for refreshment. Instead of 'have a fag' the saying was 'have a biscuit'. In the end, the catering section lost so many tins of biscuits that they were all cleared out and stored in another place. Now we had a real theatre!

It was not all fun. Since the squadron had arrived in North Africa, news from home became all important. When the men were stationed in England, mail did not have the importance that it now took on. Life seemed to revolve around the handing out of mail from home. Geoffrey Cardew continued:

> It is impossible to overestimate the importance of mail. Most people's lives revolved around the arrival or non-arrival of the post. It must have been one of the greatest single factors affecting the morale of troops in or out of the line. In my diary which

I started in March 1943, the majority of references are about who wrote to me and to whom I wrote. Some airmen would write one or two letters a day to their wives or girlfriends and then just live for the replies. In most cases all letters arrived safely, parcels too. I had one letter which took exactly a year to reach me but it turned up in the end. Regular copies of newspapers were eagerly snapped up, the most popular was the *News of the World* followed by the *Mirror*. There was the 'aerogramme' letter which came out in 1943, I think the letter itself was about quarto size, maybe a little larger. It had a space for the address and for the written matter on the same side. It was posted in the usual way but unsealed. At the base post office, it was opened, flattened and micro-filmed. The micro-film was air-mailed home where they were printed, folded and posted to the recipient.

In spite of great shortages, relatives and friends in England were able to send us parcels containing cigarettes, soap, note paper, woollen gloves, scarves and balaclavas. One snag was that if cigarettes and soap were packed together, the scent from the soap flavoured the cigarettes and made them almost unsmokable.

Though the climate of North Africa was very warm, it also had its very wet days. This restricted the amount of flying the Hudsons could do, one problem being the visibility once off the ground. At this particular time, the Sicilian campaign had begun and it fell to the aircraft of 500 Squadron to provide most of the air cover whilst the troops who were to land on the beaches of Sicily made their way by boat to the beach-heads.

A signal was received by the air officer commanding North Africa that a pack of U-boats was known to be making its way towards Sicily. Their intentions were obvious, to harass and sink the craft that were to land the men on the beaches.

Hudson flying over the Atlas Mountains between Algiers and Oran, 1943–44 (*A. D. Cummings*)

The Hudsons took off between the heavy squalls of rain and reached the patrol area on schedule. Almost immediately their radar picked up traces of submarines on the surface. Due to the swift arrival of the aircraft, none of the submarines got through to the small craft that were by now approaching the beaches. Hudson 'Q' damaged a U-boat which was finally sunk by a Ventura aircraft of No. 13 squadron. At the end of the operation, Air Vice Marshal Sir Hugh P. Lloyd flew into Blida to thank the squadron personally for enabling the Sicilian landings to take place as planned.

The awards for this particular action came through some weeks later. A DFC for Flight Lieutenant J. R. Pugh and a Mention in Despatches for Warrant Officer Hipwell amongst others.

With the majority of Hudsons now being armed with rockets, the squadron was delivering a powerful blow to the enemy. As operations continued apace, many U-boats fell victim to the increased firepower of the aircraft. It became the accepted pattern for the rockets to strike the enemy first, causing a mortal blow whereupon the Hudson would turn and deliver the depth charges in the hope of finally rupturing the plates of the U-boats. The enemy crews came to fear the sight of a Hudson bearing down upon them.

October 1943 brought the same continuation of operations. One incident however, brought much grief to many of the 500 men stationed at Blida. On Monday 18 October, a Warwick aircraft of a neighbouring squadron which shared Blida with 500 took off about noon for an air test. Geoffrey Cardew recalls:

Funeral party at Oran, 1943. (*A. D. Cummings*)

I was walking towards the flights when I noticed a Warwick flying east at only a few thousand feet between the Atlas mountains and the aerodrome. It was a warm day though not particularly bright.

There was not much flying for us on this day, training being thrust upon us by the flight sergeant. Hudson 'N' did eventually take off for a sudden strike at 13.00 hours, returning later without even seeing the enemy.

Reaching our flight area, I heard the engines of the Warwick change note. Glancing over towards the mountains I suddenly saw it spin like a stone from about 2,000 feet and crash in a plume of smoke some miles away. It appeared to just dive into the ground.

The thought of the impact turned my stomach over, especially because we knew some of the airmen on the aircraft. Our own ground crews had worked with some of them and had been speaking to them only a few minutes earlier. All eight of the crew were killed outright. Many of us attended the funeral, a very sad occasion which upset us for some time after.

Detachments of 500 Squadron had by this time been sent to another airfield some distance away from Blida. This was at Bone, another ex-French airfield. By the end of October rumours were commonplace about where various sections of the squadron would go next. Some rumours became fact, others remained rumours. John Thompson kept a diary:

19 October, Tuesday
Warm again today. Awoke feeling deadly tired. I do believe this 'orrid joint is getting me down. Nothing but perishing training flying again today. All the lads are getting really cheesed off. I am sorry to admit it but feel the morale is cracking badly. Oh for some real work for a change. No further news of the reported detachment move to Sardinia. Had job of refixing tank covering on Hudson 'N' where it was lifting in the breeze.
Finished 'Last Enemy' by Richard Hilary. It has left me strangely depressed.

On 27 October, the faithful diary again recalled:

It really is 'gen' about a squadron movement. The Blida detachment is returning en bloc to Tafaroui and rumour has it, the Bone unit is soon to be on its way to Sardinia. Rex and Harry are flying down tomorrow, whilst poor me as usual, is left to fight the rearguard action. We come off 'ops' at midnight ready for the move. After tea, hurriedly washed and went into Blida for the last time to see 'Eagle Squadron'. Really wizard film.

On 27 October, a Wednesday, most of the movement rumour became fact. A signal was received for the main part of the squadron stationed at Blida to move back to Tafaroui and the Bone unit to move to the island of Sardinia. John Thompson's diary records:

> 29 October, Friday
> Today is moving day. Up about seven and made a circuit of the block to see all the chaps were up also. Fortunately the flight commander's van is going down with us, which will ease the congestion slightly.
> Hell of a job cramming on the last kit bags and bedding rolls—the equipment lorry is an MT's nightmare!
> Collected rations and was able to scrounge a canister of tea, to start the trip with. Finally set off about nine. Not very comfortable with all the men and equipment. Our route will take in about 240 English miles. It seems endless.
> We made our first real stop on the outskirts of Miliana, near some sort of stone mines set in a steep hillside. It was quite a pretty spot and the surrounding countryside was well cultivated. We had a meal of corned beef, cheese and pickles and tried the Blida tea—as we thought, it was vile! We were, of course, surrounded by the local inhabitants pestering us for food and other things. The journey over the hills, despite the tortuous twisting of the road, had been magnificent—the scenery making North Africa seem almost worth while. The air was very cold and bracing.
> After our brief break at Miliana, we pushed on. It was rapidly getting dark so we quickly gravitated into a local hostelry where we had some community songs to Wallis's guitar. The local inhabitants were interested and appeared to enjoy listening to the 'crazy English'. Afterwards I was able to make a decent bed on the floor of the van. We set off next morning at about nine and hardly stopped again until we were about a mile from Tafaroui. After a break, we pushed on and the chaps were soon safe in their billets.

Having settled in at Tafaroui, a few days later the squadron was beset by the rumour that the move to the present airfield was all a mistake. Such was the precarious situation within the theatre in which the squadron were now operating, that it was generally felt there were too many chiefs and not enough indians! The rumour however did not become fact for all of the squadron, although it is true to say that several of the aircraft did in fact return to Blida.

December 1943 brought a change of aircraft for 500. On the 9th the squadron took over the Lockheed Venturas of No. 13 squadron who had recently departed for a new posting.

The Ventura was really a super version of the Hudson. Compared with the Hudson it had its dorsal turret positioned further forward to give a better field of fire, the underside of the fuselage was designed to give a ventral gun position and the more powerful Double Wasp engines were installed. It had only entered service with Coastal Command in the autumn, eventually replacing the Hudson entirely.

There were many members of the squadron who were sorry to see the Hudson

'A' Flight with their Venturas, North Africa 1943. (*J. Wilson*)

go, for it had served them very well indeed. It had proved a reliable aircraft and one that towards the end was fighting with a sting. Though the Ventura was a newer and more modern machine, it was a considerable time before the aircraft was accepted in the same loving way.

The chance soon came for the Ventura to be blooded with 500 Squadron a week later. The Royal Navy was suspicious that an enemy submarine was snooping around just outside Oran harbour. Calling for co-operation, a Ventura of the squadron dropped depth charges around the area and to the surprise of the Navy, the submarine broke the surface and then slowly slid back beneath the waves, mortally wounded.

As December progressed it was decided to equip the squadron with two flights of Venturas, retaining one flight of Hudsons, a total of 24 aircraft of which 16 would be Venturas.

One flight of Venturas immediately flew to a temporary detachment back to Blida. This station was the chief maintenance unit for North Africa and on various occasions, aircraft had to be flown back to Blida for major repairs. One such trip ended in disaster for one Hudson of the squadron. Geoffrey Cardew told me:

> It was about this time that there occurred a rather unfortunate accident at Blida which did not exactly endear 500 Squadron to the station. One of our Hudsons was taxying in after a patrol when, as frequently happened, it either hit a hole in the perimeter track or came off the track and went into one. The strain on the undercarriage caused the oleo leg to collapse and as a result the leg punched straight through into the wing fuel tank and up went the aircraft in flames. The crew managed to escape in safety but as the accident occurred near the dispersal, one after another of the nearby Wellingtons and Mosquitoes went up in flames. In all between 17 and 20 aircraft were

North Africa 1943 with Venturas. (*J. Wilson*)

destroyed. A signal was sent from the commanding officer of 500 to headquarters Blida requesting a replacement Hudson. The answer came back 'No—you've done enough damage already'. A few more sorties like that one and the Germans need not have troubled to try and shoot our aircraft down.

With various detachments now taking place all over North Africa, the movements of the squadron at this time were numerous. Despite the continuous upheaval the morale of the squadron, raised by the expected successes the Ventura would bring, was extremely good. The health of the men also was of the utmost importance in this hot and humid atmosphere. Generally it was very good. There were the usual heat rashes, colds and cuts and bruises but, considering some of the appalling conditions the squadron lived in, it seemed surprising that no real epidemics were ever suffered. There were of course the few who would go sick on any occasion or excuse, plus the practical joker recalled by Geoffrey Cardew:

> Our medical officer at about this time was a Squadron Leader G. Templeman. He had a lovely approach to life in general and his good humour and sympathetic manner must have had a great effect on the morale. One day one of the MT drivers called into the sick quarters with a specimen of rather muddy looking water for his inspection. The doctor asked him if he had much water like that, appalled at the state of it. The driver said: 'Five hundred gallons Sir.' 'Good God, where did you get that from,' enquired the doctor. 'It's outside Sir, I'm the driver of the water bowser!' Both men went into peels of laughter and the specimen of water remained on the shelf of the sick bay for a long time.

Although the water brought in by the bowser was alright for human consumption, the local water supply was not regarded as such. The water from the bowser was usually collected by the men in the evening. All the water bottles were filled to the brim as was every other sealed container. This water was chlorinated and made safe for drinking. Some of the men did not even trust this method and used to put more chlorine tablets into it. The colours were white to kill the germs and blue to take away the taste of the first tablet! The only snag was that it would take half an hour between the two tablets before it was considered safe to drink the water.

The usual alcoholic beverage was wine or beer. The North African wines were usually of the red or white variety and the beer of a frothy lager type. It was not very strong unless mixed with a local brandy. Then it blew the head off! The camp issue was a bottle of light ale every week if one was lucky, but local beer was always available in the NAAFI.

Tea was something else beyond the imagination of most of the squadron. Geoffrey Cardew again:

> The tea that was brewed whilst the squadron were stationed in Africa was of a most unusual colour. It appeared rather more 'rusty' in shade than a good brown pot of tea. It was usually mixed with condensed, sweetened milk, though I preferred plain water. The tea mug was one's most treasured possession. White and enamelled it took pride of place together with one's 'irons', knife, fork and spoon. These were all stamped with our service number and were the most closely guarded part of service kit. The saying was—'no mug—no drink. No irons—no eat!'
>
> The mess tins were either round or rectangular. The rectangular ones were, I think issued for overseas duty only and consisted of two parts which fitted into each other for ease of storage. The main part was for the first course and the lid for the sweet. We washed them after meals in a tank made from a 40 gallon drum cut down the centre into two semi-circular portions and filled with boiling water. By the end of the meal the washing water was cold, greasy and horrible. A swill bin was placed outside the mess tent or mess hall for uneaten food. This quite often proved a source of food supply for the locals and sometimes children would queue up for the privilege of picking out the best titbits for their own family's luncheon or supper.

Despite these conditions, it was generally understood within the command that 500 Squadron were achieving the highest record for hygiene and the smallest amount of sickness as a direct result. Being a pre-war squadron, it possessed all the advantages of a cohesive and very loyal efficient staff, proud of their work and the name of the squadron.

With the approach of another Christmas far from home, they tried to remember just what a real festive period was like. In Tafaroui the climate was very humid and a vast amount of rain seemed to fall, not at all festive. As far as possible, Christmas was celebrated in traditional style. Many parcels had arrived from people back in

England thus enabling the men to enjoy some of the usual festive fare. The NAAFI stayed open all day as did the majority of bars in Oran. A few operations took place in the afternoon but no success was scored. At the end of the day nearly everyone wondered if the next Christmas would be spent in England and at peace. All the signs were that the war was at last going our way and the enemy was on the retreat in many quarters. War however had a very funny way of suddenly rearing its ugly head again.

The 'Corsican Rats'—500 return from detachment with their Hudsons. (*J. Wilson*)

Flight huts at La Senia airfield, 1943–44. (*A. D. Cummings*)

# 11

# The Italian Job

1944 brought the good news that for the second successive year 500 Squadron had topped the General Reconnaissance squadrons' accident tables with only five accidents in 5,000 hours of flying. No mean achievement.

With various detachments still being sent all over North Africa, the tempo of the war appeared to be quickening. The military appearance of the squadron also seemed to be suffering with the continual upheaval. The dress for service in North Africa came to be a mixture of British and American uniform, as Geoffrey Cardew recalls:

> We used to dress in American-made battledress with the RAF blue flashes and boots, issue of course. The other mode of dress seemed to consist of KD shorts or trousers, either boots or shoes and occasionally gaiters. Again the flashes had to be worn but about the neck we sometimes wore scarves. With the changeable climate the dress had to suit the weather.

On 6 January 1944, the squadron moved to La Senia. This was a welcome relief to the men who by now had appeared to be getting the roughest of deals when it came to accommodation and camps.

La Senia was a large pre-war airfield. The barrack blocks were of a 'Moorish' design. They had balconies, stone floors and staircases to help keep the rooms cool in the summer. About 40 men were allocated to a room and each room had ten double bunks on each side. The alternative to this was alternate double and single bunks making about 30 only to a room. The barracks had a primitive form of heating to combat the frosts that La Senia experienced during the late winter months, however to all but a few of the men it was heaven. Geoffrey Cardew takes up the story again:

> In early 1944 we moved to La Senia, a much more impressive airfield a few miles south of Oran. There were permanent barrack blocks, large hangars and runways that

would take even the largest aircraft, including even the new B29 Superfortress, one of which landed when we were there and caused quite a stir!

The barracks were stone-floored, arcaded with a sheltered balcony on the upper floor. Beds were either two tier, wooden, or in iron-sprung singles. You had the choice of either. In both cases mosquito nets were the order of the day and we all fondly imagined we resembled virginal brides with their veils when we kipped down. I remember once fighting to get out and being smothered by the netting and in a complete state of panic and fear until I remembered to open my eyes, only to find that it was morning and I had forgotten to untuck the lower part of the netting.

The airmen's mess was large and clean with wooden tables. The food was all American rations and some of the choices were a little foreign to us. Rye bread, peanut butter and apple butter for tea. 'Yellow peril', bacon and marmalade for breakfast. Chicken or chops for lunch. Sometimes even spam or chili-con-carne. Sweet pickles, sauces, 'oleo' margarine, peanut butter and jam were always available in what to us seemed vast quantities. Even with all of this rich food, we sometimes hankered after good old bully beef and hard tack biscuits.

Wing Commander Keddie, the commanding officer, made certain that the squadron settled fully into La Senia. With various sections of the squadron on detachment all over North Africa, it was not an easy task. To all personnel, ground and air, the interest of the CO in their welfare did much for morale.

With the general theatre of the war changing, the number of anti-submarine operations began to drop. The Mediterranean was becoming a most unhealthy place for the U-boats, the RAF was taking control of the sea lanes.

Air crews and senior NCOs with a Lockheed Ventura at La Senia. (*G. Cardew*)

With the demise in U-boat activity, a regular shuttle service was introduced between La Senia and Gibraltar, making a very welcome break in the routine of patrol and reconnaissance work. With the winter weather again badly restricting operations, routine training on the ground plus the occasional parade began to become a bore.

The rest camps were something else the squadron looked forward to. La Senia offered the choice of two, one at Les Andalouses and the other at Bou Sfer. These were both minute fishing villages west of Mers El Kebir. When the holiday periods were sanctioned, the squadron personnel were able to enjoy the relaxation of bathing, doing nothing and drinking the local wine at a small bar in the evening. Since the lull in U-boat activity, the demand upon 500 was not so intense, thus enabling the majority of the men to take a leave at a rest camp. It must be remembered that during wartime normal holiday entitlements were not available. The squadrons worked year in and year out with no breaks at all except for normal roster days off duty. The rest camps proved very popular!

February 1944 brought a change of command for 500 Squadron. The very popular Wing Commander Keddie was posted to another squadron and Wing Commander Bonner arrived to lead the squadron.

With the war now on the offensive for the allies, this month saw the real start of the Italian Campaign. The Eighth Army had pushed into Calabria, nicknamed the 'toe of Italy', in September 1943. The Americans had taken Salerno the same

'La Senia Fireman', 1943. (A. D. Cummings)

month. In October the Eighth Army had moved up the Sangro river establishing the first round at Cassino in January and February 1944. Now 500 Squadron was to play a very active part in the campaign.

On 7 February a signal was received by the new commanding officer requesting that three Hudson aircraft be detached to co-operate with the Royal Navy. It was suspected that the enemy was moving his shipping from one port to another during the hours of darkness. The day reconnaissance aircraft had made very few sightings of enemy shipping, thus it was interpreted that the enemy was moving by night.

Three crews were instructed to fly the operation. Flying Officer Fuller and crew, Flying Officer Alan and crew and Warrant Officer Munday and crew. They took off from La Senia on 7 February and landed at Gibraltar the same day.

On the morning of the 8th, Flying Officer Fuller, who was in charge of the detachment, attended a conference at No. 2 General Reconnaissance headquarters. Feeling somewhat out of place, Fuller noted that he was the only Air Force officer amongst many high-ranking Royal Navy officers.

The briefing began with a detailed account of the enemy's movements in the operational area. With the suggestion that enemy ships were moving by night, the Hudsons were detailed to patrol from the area of Nice to Vigi and report any shipping seen outside the port area after the time of darkness. This was required because the Navy was unable, during the hours of darkness, to cover the required area. It was intended that the Navy would place motor torpedo boats in position at various points along the aircraft patrol routes so that when a sighting was made by the Hudsons, they would be in a position to intercept and deliver an attack.

Practice bombs, La Senia, 1944. Left to right—LAC George Mortimer, Sgt Harry Pink, Cpl Geoff Cardew. (*G. Cardew*)

The plan was carefully worked out and the crews of the Hudsons were told to fly as close as possible to the coast and make the best of the moonlight to illuminate any target the airborne radar of the Hudson might indicate. The pilots were briefed to fly as low as possible to reduce the chance of enemy radar picking them up. Fifteen minutes was the maximum time ordered in which to fly a steady course. At the end of this period, the aircraft was to change course to the general direction of Corsica and begin the pattern all over again.

The patrols began on 10 February but very soon proved a strain for just three crews to undertake. With a signal sent via the officer commanding the General Reconnaissance squadrons, three more crews from 500 Squadron were detailed to assist Flying Officer Fuller. These were the crews of Squadron Leader Garton, Warrant Officer McLennan and Flight Sergeant Clela.

The operations continued night after night without much success. The weather conditions were sometimes very bad thus making the flying very bumpy. The Hudson was not really suitable for low level night flying. Its radar could not detect the channel between the Isle of Elba and the Italian mainland, which is a distance of less than five miles.

It was also found that if the aircraft flew above 1,000 feet the problem of freezing conditions arose, both for crew and aircraft. If a target was pinpointed on the screen and the flares were needed for identification, the aircraft had to climb to 2,000 feet in order to release the flares. At this height not only was the problem of icing up apparent but heavy cumulous clouds were encountered as well. To the crew member in the upper turret it must have seemed like a nightmare. He had no heating at all to relieve his frozen limbs.

The aircraft and crews however carried out a full operational detachment, unfortunately without much success in sighting enemy movements.

When the detachment came to an end, Squadron Leader Garton, commander of the air and ground crews who carried out these duties, placed upon record the exemplary way in which all the personnel had carried out their duties. On no occasion did the detachment fail to meet its flying commitments.

Back at La Senia, the remainder of the squadron were experiencing their own particular problems. John Thompson recorded in his diary:

11th February—Friday

A little heavy this morning. Weather windy and cold with great banks of threatening cloud piling up. Fortunately no rain but remained bitterly cold throughout the day. No flying. After tea went down to La Senia with Bud to fetch our clean laundry. Afterwards met up with a bunch of the boys and adjourned to our favourite abode to celebrate Herbie Loader's birthday. Jim Wallis and Jock Ramsey were there complete with guitar and violin. Beaucoup music and song.

Visited the egg eating shop and finally disappeared into the local cinema for a stage show. Returned to billets about a quarter to twelve. Quite an enjoyable evening.

12th February—Saturday

Beautiful day today—cold, bright and bracing. Still no flying. This job is really getting monotonous, only the bullshit remains consistent.

Visited pay accounts and was acquainted with the glad tidings that I have just over £19 in credit—what ho.

14 February—Monday

Cold most of the day. Flight now sadly depleted with some in Corsica and some on detachment elsewhere. Usual binding colour hoisting parade with the inevitable attendant loss of time. Went into Oran in the evening for ice cream and suitable liquid refreshment. Went to the pictures afterwards and was lucky enough to get a lift right to the block door in a posh staff car . . . and so to bed.

So the fifth year of war moved on. The constant movement of men and machines to different detachments, whether for long or short periods, broke some of the monotony for air and ground crews. With these movements, some of the advance ground crew travelled as passengers in the aircraft to enable it to function as a complete unit immediately upon reaching the detachment airfield. Though the ground crew cared for their charges in a loving way, when it came to flying in them they did not feel so enthusiastic, Geoffrey Cardew among them:

Another interesting detachment was to Bone when we were equipped with Venturas. We took off from La Senia on a lovely day, a little cloudy but clear and bright. As this detachment was to be of a short duration, I chose to travel in one of the aircraft. We circled over the airfield, climbed to 1,000 feet and set off. As we approached the coast the nose suddenly went down and we dived towards a small speck in the sea. I could not really see much because I was in the fuselage but I remember the aircraft pulling out of the dive leaving me wondering just where my stomach was!

Being absolutely petrified of flying I assumed the worst, that I was going to crash in the sea. However, I was assured that everything was alright and that the pilot had spotted what he assumed to be a body floating in the water. It turned out to be just floating wood.

The fear of flying made sure that I was able to go off to sleep quite easily as a form of escape. There I was, lying on kitbags snoring away when I was suddenly wakened by the navigator pulling my arm and shouting 'pump away' at the same time pointing to a handle on the internal 40 gallon oil tank in the fuselage. I also noticed that he was struggling with his parachute. I won't say I panicked, but I never pumped so hard in my life, thinking that we were an ace away from disaster. My relief was undisguised when I realised what was happening. On the Ventura it was normal procedure to pump oil from the emergency tank periodically during the flight, particularly when there was a full load of depth charges and auxiliary fuel tanks on the wings. This is what was happening. The navigator was looking for his measuring instrument which somehow had got mixed up in his parachute pack. Sweet relief!

We landed safely, immediately checked that all our aircraft were in order and then looked for somewhere to sleep. We were directed to a Nissen hut and told to kip down there. No beds, a granite chipping floor and two or three lengths of corrugated iron. First of all I tried the corrugated iron, two or three blankets and a groundsheet just do not make an adequate mattress. About midnight I had really had enough of that. Trying the granite chipping was not exactly heaven either. Finally, weary, I grabbed all my kit and crept back into the Ventura. My gasmask made a super pillow and snuggling in next to the belly guns was a great improvement on the bare hut with its absolute lack of any amenities. We weren't at Bone long but I do remember vividly helping to refuel the oil tanks on the aircraft.

The Ventura required 40 gallons of oil and the supply was in one pint cans that had to be opened by hand and then passed into the aircraft to be poured into a funnel. Filling the petrol tanks was much easier. We used 10 gallon tins because there was no petrol bowser available. However all of this had to be done by filtering the petrol through chamois leather stretched across a funnel to exclude any water that might have got in by accident. Thank goodness there was plenty of Arab labour available. At least it was cheap!

Though the anti-submarine operations had fallen to a minimum, the occasional sweep was still on the programme. On 22 February 1944, Ventura 'M' was ordered on such a sweep to cover the distance between La Senia and Blida. The crew were Flying Officer F. S. Knighton, Sergeant Potter, Flight Sergeant Avril CSM, Warrant Officer Campbell and Warrant Officer Biglow.

The aircraft took off late afternoon in fair weather and performed a very uneventful operation. A contact was made in the water but the size of the echo denoted that it was not an enemy submarine. Landing back at La Senia at 20.15 hours, 'M' was taxying back to the flight dispersal when the port wheel ran into a rather large hole in the perimeter track.

Coming down heavily on the fuselage, the two external tanks burst into flames and in no time it had reached the entire aircraft. In rather a hurry, the crew left the aircraft, all of them running to safety and reaching it just in time to see Ventura 'M', their beloved aircraft, disintegrate into a million pieces!

News of the war back home in England very often found its way to 500 Squadron in North Africa. The letters from loved ones and relations told of the progress of the war on the home front. The way the Royal Air Force was clearing the skies over England of the Luftwaffe; the way in which the Army was pushing the enemy further and further back and the inevitable thoughts that the war would be over by Christmas 1944. They did not tell of the horror of the enemy bombing on the cities or the fact that many of them knew that a new and terrible weapon was about to be unleashed upon them. All of this would have only caused anxiety to the men of the squadron and would not have allowed them to concentrate fully on the matter of defeating the enemy.

500 squadron air and ground crews at La Senia, 1944. (*A. D. Cummings*)

# The Italian Job

On the operational side in England, the truth was that the first few months of 1944 were heavily occupied with the misfortunes of Bomber Command. Together with the plans for the coming landings in Normandy plus the watch for pilotless aircraft and long range rockets it would appear that RAF units stationed abroad were not suffering as much as those back in the homeland. It is true to say that each theatre of war presents its own particular problems whether in England or in some foreign country. This was no less applicable to 500 than to any other squadron.

In March, more detachments took place at Borizzo and Blida. With the Italian Campaign gathering momentum, one of the last U-boat sinkings fell sour on 500 Squadron. Geoffrey Cardew recalls:

Early in 1944 I was in the process of remustering from fitter/armourer gun to fitter/armourer general. I was under the watchful eye of Sergeant Harry Pink. As part of the training I was allowed to assist in 'bombing up' and all the other operations involved in being a fitter/armourer bombs. Corporal 'Zoot-suit' Jackson and I worked together as we were both in the same trade and were in the process of retraining.

One evening we were on duty crew and had bombed up and serviced 'U' Uncle, a Ventura which was on standby. She was sent off on a 'flap' during the night and was not due back till the next morning. When she returned just before dawn it was with the exciting news that she had sunk a submarine.

The story was that for some while a German submarine had been cornered by the Navy just off Oran. As 'U' came over to help in the search, the craft suddenly surfaced. The navigator immediately reacted, pressed the bomb 'tit' and down went the depth charges. There was a great shower of spray and the aircraft left the submarine sinking.

We were thrilled over the news but imagine our horror when upon inspecting the aircraft for any damage, the bomb doors were opened only to find one depth charge still hanging up and fully primed! Panic stations.

By now however, Jacko and I were off duty so went back to the billet, had a shave, wash and breakfast and then set off to Oran for a day's 'Empire building' as we commonly called it.

When we returned to camp, we found that the armament officer was nearly bursting a blood vessel looking for the armourers who had armed 'U' Uncle with her depth charges. He was assuming that the hang-up was due to our inexperience. Feeling sheepish, we went down to the dispersal area only to find that to our relief it had been proved that the hang-up was due to the navigator accidentally kicking off one of the bomb panel switches. We were in the clear! Next day checking the bomb racks, the fault reoccurred. A quick chat to the electrician and a faulty bomb release mechanism was repaired. Still their fault, not ours! After all we did get the sub! I believe the Navy was furious at losing the craft to the Air Force so we were only allowed a claim a ½ sinking.

## The Italian Job

On 9 March 1944 at 12.59 hours, one of the last air sea rescue missions was carried out by the squadron. The Operations Records Book faithfully recorded:

> La Senia—9 March 12.59 hours. Ventura D carried out ASR search for dinghy 50 miles N from Cape Chenour to Cape Bengut. During patrol gunner thought he saw body in water.

To think that so much triumph and so much despair had come the way of the squadron in its past and present existence yet the last air sea rescue operations should demand such a little mention on the pages of history that were being written at this time.

To alleviate much of the boredom of routine work within the squadron, many of the personnel of 500 took to smoking cigarettes. The standard issue of 50 English were free but more cigarettes could be purchased in the NAAFI, though these were of American origin. Tins of tobacco were also available, these were again of American origin and were in oval-shaped tins. They were known by the non-American name of 'Prince Albert' and consisted of a very powdery and dry mixture. Some was even chewed! The local cigarettes were called 'Victory V's but even the Arabs refused to smoke these, which said much about their contents, and they were therefore left well alone.

Although it was now approaching summer, the weather was not as expected. Low cloud and terrific winds again hampered many missions. Those who managed to get off on operations frequently came back without seeing the target or the enemy. On 1 June 1944 Ventura 'B' took off from La Senia on one of the last anti-submarine patrols for the squadron. The crew were Flight Sergeant Wolfe, Flight Sergeant Herbener, Sergeant Grittins, Warrant Officer Thacker and Warrant Officer Kriklewicz, one of the Polish men serving in the squadron. Heading towards Gibraltar, the patrol area was set between La Senia and a point just east of the rock. The weather was poor with very low cloud, barely enabling the crew to see the surface of the water. Just a few hours into the operation, the crew requested a return to base, they had seen absolutely nothing. Permission was granted and a very disappointed crew and aircraft returned to La Senia. Further evidence of frustrated operations during June were recorded in the Operations Record Book:

> La Senia—June 44—The month of June has been one of the quietest on record for operational flying for the squadron. The high command have thought it unnecessary to escort the majority of convoys passing through the area.
>
> Very few anti-U-boat patrols were flown from La Senia as part of the general training programme for new crews. The work of the Gibraltar detachment has consisted of anti-U-boat patrols and anti-submarine reconnaissance.
>
> During the month the ground crews of No. 27 (South African Air Force) squadron arrived on the station and have been assisting our own ground crews. Also during the

month of June, three aircraft were despatched to 156 maintenance unit at Blida for major inspections. These aircraft were Ventura FP 662, Ventura FP652 and Ventura FP628.

The only good news about June was that a former 500 Squadron officer who had served at Manston in the halcyon days of 1936 had been appointed commanding officer of 500 Squadron. With Wing Commander Bonner returning to England, Wing Commander C. E. A. Garton was promoted to command.

With June gone and July bringing a promise of more action for the squadron, it came as a great shock when the rumours about the future of 500 Squadron began to abound in every corner of the station. Like a plague, it travelled around La Senia. '500 to disband? Surely it cannot be true. Why, when, where!' Had someone higher up made a big mistake?

Sadly the rumour proved to be true. After thirteen years of devoted and conscientious service to the Royal Air Force, the squadron was to disband. From the humble beginnings in 1931, flying Vickers Virginias at Manston to the present day service in North Africa flying Venturas, the squadron had achieved a splendid record. The signs were in Europe that the war was at last drawing to a close, hence the reductions in RAF squadrons.

On 1 July 1944, all ranks were assembled on the sandy parade ground at La Senia. Calling the parade to attention, the parade Sergeant saluted the commanding officer Wing Commander Garton who then mounted a small rostrum in the centre of the ground. Standing the men at ease, the commanding officer addressed his squadron. He outlined briefly to them the past history of the squadron, stating that owing to the lack of general reconnaissance work, the squadron indeed was being disbanded forthwith. This was being accelerated so much that he now had the names of aircrew personnel who were to be classed as 'tour expired', this meaning the return to a station in the United Kingdom pending their release from the service. The remainder of the aircrew would be posted to No. 22 South African Air Force Squadron at Gibraltar or to No. 27 South African Air Force Squadron at La Senia.

Turning to the ground crews of 500 Squadron, Wing Commander Garton recalled the excellent work done by the ranks. The majority of ground crews would be returning to England whereupon they would be posted to other squadrons within the command.

Having given the squadron the bad news, Wing Commander Garton now turned to other matters. Again, briefly outlining the history of the squadron he paid tribute to all personnel who had served with 500 through the hardest times. He hoped that those posted to other squadrons would maintain the good example and comradeship that had been set by 500. If it were possible when the war was ended, he hoped that a squadron reunion would be held to reunite them all. When his address was finished, the commanding officer hoped that God would bless them all.

So it was, after all, true and not just rumour. 500 Squadron was to disband. Further indications of disbandment came when the air officer commanding Sir Hugh Pugh Lloyd visited the squadron the same afternoon. Again emphasising the past history and the future of General Reconnaissance squadrons in general, the air officer commanding said that he hoped to post as many auxiliary members of the squadron as possible back home. He was unable to say to just which squadrons they would be posted or on what type of work they would be engaged. He then, as the commanding officer had done, thanked all members for their support and devotion to duty.

And so 500 Squadron began the run-down. It was natural that an air of apathy settled on the personnel. They could not see just why it had to be their squadron that was being disbanded. Having done stirling work for the command and achieving much success, it came as a bitter blow to the men.

Over the next week, the task of documentation and completing an inventory on the equipment was completed. Orders were promulgated to advise on the various postings throughout the squadron.

On 11 July 1944, the aircraft and all of the equipment were officially handed over to No. 27 (SAAF) Squadron which was to take the place of 500 at La Senia. Many aircrew were posted forthwith and a number of the auxiliaries returned to England.

The final curtain had fallen on No. 500 (County of Kent) Squadron—Royal Auxiliary Air Force.

# 12

# Desert Air Force

It will never really be known if it were an act of God or whether somebody at the headquarters of the Mediterranean Coastal Air Force had got his sums wrong and suddenly realised it in the nick of time. Whatever it was, before the entire squadron had left La Senia, a signal was received giving notice of the reforming of the squadron. More than that, they were to convert to the Martin Baltimore, a heavily armed light bomber aircraft. The squadron was to operate under the command of the Desert Air Force, operating from La Senia.

Imagine the sort of stir that this news caused. Amid great jubilation for the former members of the squadron left behind, the newer men posted in wondered what on earth there was to celebrate. Suddenly a new air of excitement surrounded the squadron.

By 1 August the reforming was complete, except for the aircraft which had not yet materialised. Considerable difficulty was experienced in collecting much of the equipment which had been handed to No. 27 Squadron. Orders were again changed and the squadron was instructed to proceed to Italy.

With the reforming of the squadron came a new commanding officer, Wing Commander H. N. Garbet.

The squadron was ordered to Pescara, a little town on the Adriatic coast. There they would find the Baltimore aircraft that they were to convert to. To the aircrew of the new squadron the prospect of the Baltimore was exciting. The Royal Air Force was using this aircraft exclusively in the Mediterranean, operating them both by day and night. It had played a very prominent part during the North African offensive and was now being used extensively in the Italian Campaign. Powered by two Wright double row Cyclone engines, the aircraft had an all metal stressed skin construction with a maximum speed of 302 mph at 11,000 feet. With a maximum bomb load of 2,000 lb the armament consisted of four 0.303 guns in the wings, two or four 0.303 guns in a dorsal turret and two 0.30 guns in the ventral position. It also had provision for four fixed rear firing 0.30 guns. The whole aircraft packed a formidable punch.

The process of getting ready to move now took preference over everything else at La Senia. By 21 August the squadron had received its orders and was ready to move. The ground crew, which accounted for the main bulk of the squadron, embarked on the liner *Villa d'Oran*, a luxury French liner that had now been converted as a troopship.

On 23 August she sailed from Algiers for Taranto, the first leg of a very long journey. Escorted by a destroyer and a frigate, the liner slipped out of Algiers at nightfall. The accommodation was rather cramped and the ship was very full. Despite these conditions, the food was very well organised and plenty was available.

After a very uneventful journey, the *Villa d'Oran* docked at Taranto. The squadron thanked the members of the crew and disembarked to cover the rest of the journey by train.

Whilst the sea journey had been tolerable, the train journey was not. No prior arrangements had been made for the squadron to continue its journey to Pescara. Somewhere along the line the system had failed. This meant that the men had to remain at the sidings six or seven hours until the next available train was found. The sidings offered no shelter at all from the blistering heat that was prevalent at this time of year. The ground crews could only sit around and sweat it out. Two totally inadequate meals were served consisting of bully beef and stale biscuits. These were served in such a way that they were open to attack from the millions of flies that seemed to be attracted to bully beef.

At 20.30 hours, an Italian railman informed the senior NCO that a train would be arriving in about fifteen minutes. When it did arrive it consisted of cattle trucks only. Still, many of them thought, let's just get out of this hell hole. After a lot of fussing by Italian officials, the train departed from Taranto.

The stop and start journey continued throughout the night until 06.00 hours the following morning. With a final gasp of steam, the train drew into a siding and hot water was made available for tea.

Never had a pot of tea been so welcome. A break of about one hour allowed the men to stretch their legs. The serious business of washing and bathing was conducted by courtesy of the Italian State Railway. The sidings happened to have a water hose for replenishing the water in the locomotives boilers. The height of this apparatus was just right to enable it to become an instant shower! In the morning heat, even at six o'clock, anything refreshing was welcome.

The necessary human functions performed, the train was again boarded and it proceeded on its way.

The second stop of the day was made at Salerno where arrangements were far better organised than at Taranto. All personnel received their first hot meal in 24 hours, the entire contents proving most edible—even by Italian standards. With Naples now only 30 miles away it would not be long before they reached more permanent accommodation. However, the 30 miles took six hours with many stops due to the effects of bombing. With the summer sun now directly overhead, many of the men succumbed to heat stroke and were very glad when the train finally slid slowly into Naples Central, and they were able to disembark.

The squadron commander, Wing Commander Garbett, who had flown on ahead to make arrangements for the squadron, was waiting on the platform to welcome them to Naples. Geoffrey Cardew will never forget that dreadful train journey:

> We arrived in Naples from Taranto by train—cattle trucks in fact. As long as the weather was good it was bearable. The trains travelled at a very leisurely pace and we could either sit on the floor on our ground sheets or dangle our legs out of the door and admire the view. It is surprising how quickly we accustomed ourselves to the most extraordinary situations and it never took long to get 'organised', a term that means making the most of every available object in view to further the comfort and well-being of airmen.
>
> It was in fact bitterly cold at night and we huddled together in greatcoats and blankets to keep warm. At about six in the morning we stopped at Potenza for breakfast. I remember vividly the sight of dozens of airmen rushing about and looking like Arabs wrapped in blankets trying to grab what little food there was. Others were rushing up to the engine with their mugs for hot water to make tea.
>
> It was late afternoon when we reached what we thought was the industrial area of southern Italy. A large slag heap, grey and dirty, came into view. We were very

Shower time for 500 Squadron *en route* from Taranto to Naples on the Adriatic coast, 1944–45. (*G. Cardew*)

puzzled and racked our brains as to where we might be. The surrounding area was also filthy and there were a few factory-like buildings and chimney stacks that gave the impression of a mining district. In the foreground were vines loaded with grapes, the brilliant green leaves contrasting with the sombre background.

And then the penny dropped! We were looking at the world famous Vesuvius. It was such an anti-climax that we collapsed in hysterical laughter. Tears rolled down our cheeks as we chugged past this insignificant dirty heap of slag.

Soon we reached Naples itself and here we were met by fantastic destruction caused mostly by our own bombers. There were burnt-out carriages, torn up railway lines, bomb craters and rubble everywhere. Massive railway engines literally standing on their ends, others split open like tin cans. It was the first time we had actually seen the results of RAF bombing operations. To be fair, most of the damage was on military installations and although many blocks of flats were heaps of rubble, these were mostly in the dock area and the town itself was relatively unscathed.

With the squadron's arrival in Naples, life took on a luxurious air. Geoffrey Cardew continues:

Our billets were in houses commandeered from well-to-do Italians in Portici, close to the Royal Palace about five miles from the town of Naples. They were cool and clean, all the rooms were tiled, floors and walls, to temper the fierce summer heat. Local Italian girls swept and washed the rooms daily and for a short while we lived a life of comparative luxury. No dusting, no work to do and bags of time off to visit Naples and the local bars!

We messed in the Royal Palace and I well remember the long queues of airmen standing along one wall on which everyone who had been through the transit camp had written their names and unit numbers. All the chaps wrote their names on this wall together with a pseudo-latin motto 'Nil Bastardo Carburundum—Don't let the bastards grind you down'! I wonder what happened to that splendid example of graffiti. It was probably painted over as soon as the RAF left.

The NAAFI in Naples was situated in the Royal Palace itself and it was with great pride that one wandered up the magnificent marble staircase and ate one's tea and wads in the ballrooms where Nelson and Lady Hamilton had been received by the King and Queen of Naples during the Napoleonic wars. The terrace of the Palace gave a magnificent view of the Bay of Naples with Vesuvius in the background. It was unbelievably 'picture postcard' but some small compensation for the reluctant heroes of 500 Squadron who had so recently been living in the squalor of cattle trucks and troopships.

With the squadron now well rested and Naples being fed up with them, on 12 September 1944 at 08.00 hours, the party left for Pescara by road. With the adjutant leading the convoy, good progress was made on inferior roads. By 14

September after a very long and uneventful journey, the squadron reached Pescara. It was found to be a quite well equipped airfield but the surface for flying left much to be desired.

With the lateness of the hour and too tired even to look at the Baltimores they had inherited from 55 Squadron, the men had time only for a hot meal before finding themselves a bed place at the new camp.

Next morning came the crunch. Due to the heavy operational programme with which 55 Squadron had been entrusted, the Baltimores were found to be in poor condition. Out of the entire complement of aircraft only four were found to be serviceable, the rest of them required major servicing.

Glad to be back at a residential station, the ground crews immediately tackled the other aircraft with great gusto and the end of September saw all of the aircraft in service in tip-top condition.

And so, having arrived and settled in Pescara, a full programme of intensive training began, both for aircrews and ground crews. The inevitable changes took place in the squadron. Squadron Leader Reece, the commander of 'A' flight was posted out and Squadron Leader Evers arrived to take over the duties of flight commander. The conversion to the Baltimore took preference over all other duties.

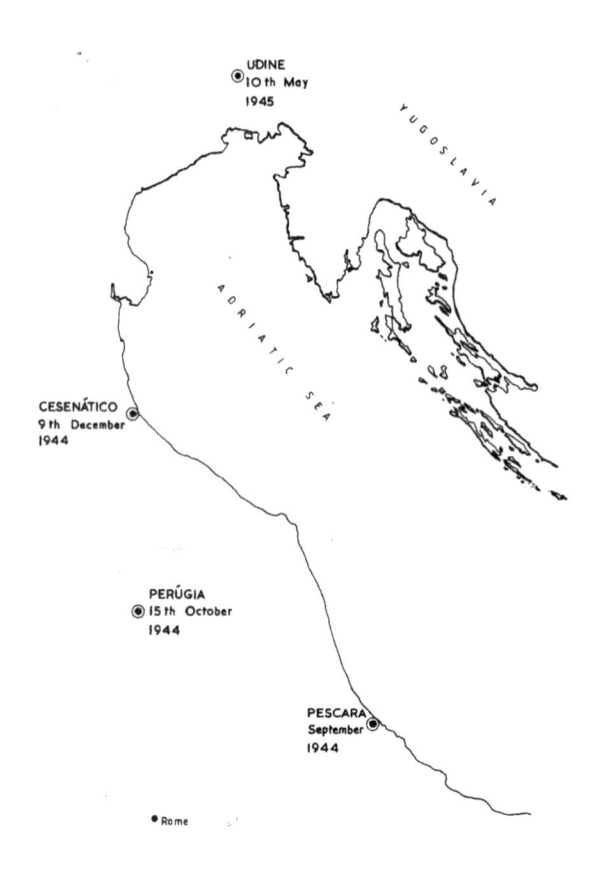

Pescara Airfield, September 1944. The tents were used as billets. (*G. Cardew*)

With the end of summer fast approaching, the weather began to change rapidly. No more was the hot sun tanning the bodies of the squadron. Heavy rain and winds replaced this and the rather unsuitable flying surface became a bog, causing the aircraft to become stuck to the tops of their wheels. From the 28th the rain was continuous, keeping the airfield unserviceable until the end of the month, thus delaying all training and conversion to the new aircraft.

The only highlight of the month was for the officers when they held a small party in the mess. The lady guests included Canadian nurses and members of a touring ENSA company. Whilst it was really a party to welcome the squadron to Pescara, it ended as a departure party, for the next day half of the personnel were ordered to leave the airfield with its unsuitable flying conditions and proceed to an undisclosed destination.

A list of personnel to make up the advance party was promulgated and on 28 November they left Pescara for the last time. Tents were issued for the journey by road and although tent life was not new to many members of the squadron, the conditions were. Torrential rain seemed to follow the party to the new destination making life very difficult. The lamps for the tents were constantly out due to the continual trickle of water running down the sides. Usually these lamps, made of a combination of cigarette tins, paraffin and string, were surprisingly efficient until, that is, they met the Italian rains.

Progress was very slow for the advance party. The new station had now been named as Perugia, an airfield similar in size to Pescara. It was hoped that the new base would afford better and more facilities for a continuous training programme.

Food for the party was cooked at every stop on the journey, often under extreme conditions. This was considered better because much of the journey to Perugia was

Baltimore 'V' Victor, Italy 1944–45. (*G. Cardew*)

over open country with no sign of habitation. However you can never really please a hungry airman like Geoffrey Cardew:

> Rations were usually adequate and our cook, Sergeant Duddleston and his staff always managed to produce meals under the most difficult circumstances. One famous saying was that there are a hundred and one ways of cooking bully beef and HE KNOWS ONE! We had bully beef cold in slices, bully beef stew, bully beef fritters, bully beef fried and bully beef curry but owing to circumstances beyond our control, there was always bully beef!

A few days later the advance party arrived at Perugia, the rest following later. With the aircraft already at the airfield, the next morning dawned bright and clear and training commenced with a new vengeance.

In order to make up for time lost at Pescara, the crews were subjected to flying training both morning and afternoon. Flights consisted of cross-country and bombing practice on the local ranges, much to the annoyance of the local villagers.

The bombing practice became so bad and noisy for the locals that a deputation of elderly residents marched on the station headquarters to protest. With Baltimores thundering overhead at near roof-top level, they tried to make their point about their primitive houses shaking and pieces falling off. Whilst nothing could be done to alleviate the position for these unfortunate people, they were shown around the station, while the position of the RAF was fully explained and then taken for a meal in the mess. Thus they left in a far better frame of mind than when they came and nothing more was ever heard about the noise.

Training continued at a furious pace. The Italian Campaign was reaching its conclusion and 500 wanted to be a part of the last thrust. Rumours were that the

Over the Adriatic, Martin 187 Baltimores, 1944–45. (*G. Cardew*)

war would be over by Christmas and the squadron still had not blooded their Baltimores.

All of this changed when orders were received for training to cease and the squadron to be placed on an operational footing. 500 was ordered from Perugia to Cesenatico, an airfield again on the Adriatic coast but a considerable journey to the north. Here it was hoped that the squadron would again be in combat with the enemy.

The ground and administration crews left Perugia on 1 December and after another considerably tiring journey arrived at the new base. On the 9th the aircraft and crews left Perugia and arrived at Cesenatico the same day. Upon arrival a new sound was heard over the whole area. This was the continuous booming of guns indicating the close proximity of the front, something that 500 had not experienced since North Africa. Strict orders were issued reminding the men that lights and fires after dark had to be screened lest the enemy saw them.

One overall advantage however was the airfield surface. This was a definite improvement on Pescara and Perugia, being of sandy soil with little or no mud in sight. Somerfeld strip was laid on the sandy surface ensuring that the aircraft did not sink into the sand. At last the squadron felt it was to see some more action. John Thompson wrote in his diary:

Saturday 9th 1944—Cesenatico. Things began to materialise today—had warning signal in reference to the aircraft which eventually came on the circuit about 11.50 hours.

All the machines made good landings but we had quite a flap getting three on to the hard standings in some cases. The operation necessitated plenty of pushing and shoving. A lot of trouble with our pet aversions—the 'bowsers'—but finally managed

A Baltimore lands on a rain-soaked airfield in Italy. Note metal stripping laid on airfield surface.

to get them all snugged down for the night. A round dozen of 'A' flight airmen came up with the aircraft which gave them the afternoon off to settle down in their tents.

Sunday 10th—Burst of activity on the 'drome today. Other squadrons took part in some operations but we spent day in thoroughly checking our machines.

Squadron Leader Bull and Squadron Leader Evers took off in 'V' and 'F' respectively for a 'looksee' and to check up on the bomb line. 'V' came back with some shrapnel in the engine but this wasn't found out until later when the aircraft was due for a minor service.

Twelve SAF (South African Air Force) aircraft came back shot up by 'flak', three having to go into the bays for repairs. Plenty of excitement in the squadron as we bomb up for our first big 'do' tomorrow. Thrills mixed with chills on the part of the aircrews.

In the morning of 11 December, 500 Squadron mounted its first operation of the month. It was intended to put twelve aircraft up but in the event only ten were fully serviceable by the time the squadron was due to depart. The two that did not take part were 'W' which had gashed a tyre on the metal stripping and 'F' which was serviced too late to take off with the rest. All the aircraft returned safely some hours later, the only damage being inflicted on Squadron Leader Bull's aircraft 'U' for Uncle. This turned out to be a flak hole through the aileron. As soon as the aircraft landed they were checked and refuelled ready for the next day's operations. Now there was to be no let up on the action.

Next day, however, the weather turned bad. Thick fog blanketed the front causing a halt to all operations. This was an ideal time for the ground crews to get the Baltimores in top line condition ready for the next assault. Congratulations were received from Group headquarters for the squadron's share in the sorties that were carried out yesterday and a formal welcome back into the operational theatre, so sadly missed by 500 over the past six months.

The 13th, 14th and 15th of December saw no change. Still the fog prevented operations taking place. On the 16th the weather finally broke. John Thompson's diary:

> Saturday 16th. Weather still deadly but sky brightened considerably towards noon. The operations gong sounded about 13.30 and we rushed joyously into the fray.
>
> Plenty of activity everywhere on the 'drome. Aircraft going off in all directions but we have a target all our own. We learn by devious routes that it is a heavy gun site near Castel Bologna.
>
> To our relief we get twelve aircraft off without mishap—not even a burst tail wheel but 'B' flight's formation was very straggly.
>
> Aircraft returned about 16.00 hours and to our dismay we see one machine is missing from the 'B' flight group. When the aircraft land we see that all are damaged more or less by 'flak', it has obviously been a hot job. At least two of 'A' flight's machines are seriously holed, 'D' and 'J'.
>
> We now know the missing aircraft to be 'W', Flight Sergeant Snow and crew. The machine was hit by flak over the target, one engine being severely damaged. The aircraft failed to make base on one engine finally crashing 5 kms north of Cervia in some mud flats and burnt out. Flight Sergeant Snow is OK, Flight Sergeant Thomas slightly injured, Flight Sergeants Hedley and Messenger have had it.

As soon as the news of the crash reached the station headquarters at Cesenatico, the squadron medical officer and the engineering officer drove to the scene of the crash. Some trouble was experienced in finding the location as no information was readily available as to the exact spot. Eventually local people helped and they reached the scene to find a most horrific sight.

The locals had managed to drag three of the crew from the burning aircraft and had taken them to the local hospital. They informed the medical officer that one of the crew had perished in the holocaust, this being Warrant Officer Messenger. The full story evolved that the Baltimore had received a direct hit in the port engine causing the aircraft to be uncontrollable. Flight Sergeant Snow had tried in vain to keep the plane in the air but eventually had been forced to crash land close to Cervia.

Feeling that nothing more could be done by remaining at the scene of the crash, the two officers returned to Cesenatico. The next day the commanding officer, Wing Commander Garbet, returned from a visit from the 5th General hospital bringing the news that Flight Sergeant Hedley had died without gaining consciousness. Flight Sergeants Snow and Thomas were not seriously injured but were suffering mainly from shock. The whole squadron mourned the loss of the two men and the entire crash had a profound effect on the squadron.

On the 17th, 18th, 19th and 20th of December the weather again prevented operations over the enemy lines. The situation however called for more flying

Baltimore 'Q' for Queenie.

training around the base even though operations were cancelled. John Thompson's diary:

> 17th December—Once more the weather has clamped down to stop ops. It has been decided by the powers that be, that if the weather persisted in holding up operational flying the opportunity would be seized to do some local practice. To that end we sent up 'R', 'T' and 'N' on formation but did not bother to debomb them. Stormy meeting at night dealing with the Christmas period. The news is a bit shaky on the Western Front. The Germans have thrust forward 30 miles into the American lines.
>
> 18th December—The 'ops' gong went today at 08.30. After much flap and excitement the weather clamped down and it was all cancelled. Very rough night with showers of light snow blowing. Bitter piercing wind almost creasing us.

On 18 December, Warrant Officer Messenger was buried at Cesenatico with full military honours. With the coffin draped in the Union Jack, the funeral party was made up mainly of personnel from 500 Squadron. It was a melancholy scene, an English burial service set in a wilderness of sand and desolation. A rifle party fired a volley of shots over the coffin and the squadron padre conducted a simple service. As the sun dipped toward the horizon the last post was sounded and the party marched back to base.

With mid-December approaching, the weather took its toll of cancelled operations. It was continually overcast and now bitterly cold. The tented accommodation at the airfield was found to be totally inadequate for the amount of frost experienced. No amount of extra blankets could keep the intense cold at bay. With Christmas fast approaching, the best that could be said was that it was seasonable. John Thompson's diary:

> 24th December—Weather still bitterly cold and overcast. Went to pay accounts at lunch time and after waiting patiently whilst sundry officers pushed into the queue,

was able to ensure that the 11,800 lire I drew hadn't put me in debt. Had reasonable binge in the mess and visited some of the boys with a drink or two.

Christmas Day 1944—Weather still cold but it has cleared up somewhat. Spent deadly morning at dispersal, came to lunch as sky cleared. Sure enough the 'gong' went at 13.30 hours and we had to scamper for it. Bags of flap and panic, finally got the whole 12 on the runway and then the whole job was scrubbed. Curses! Foiled again! Got back to tent about 16.00 hours, did not visit airmen's dinner—had a slice of cake and a cup of tea and then went to the officers mess for a drink, where I had quite a long chat to the CO and was able to spread on a bit of the good work.

Later returned to the mess in a semi-drunken condition and enjoyed a nice big dinner. Not being in the mood for much drinking was not too late to bed. Thus another Christmas!

And so the sixth Christmas of war passed quickly by. The hangovers of the celebrations were rudely shattered on the 26th when the weather was found to be clear and bright and operations were hastily arranged. Briefing of the aircrews took place at 07.30 hours with the 'gong' sounding at the same time to arouse the ground crews. Many of the aircraft proved stubborn at starting due to excessive cold and lack of engine run-ups. Eventually twelve aircraft were made available and the operation was on.

The morning raid was on the supply and bomb dumps at Imola. Both 'A' and 'B' flights of the squadron took part and all machines returned safely to Cesenatico. No opposition or flak was met on the raid and the dumps were left in flames and total confusion. The whole operation was a great success.

The same aircraft were rapidly turned round, rearmed and refuelled and were airborne again by 14.00 hours. This time the target was the marshalling yards at Conegliano. The visibility was again excellent and the yards were left in smouldering ruin.

Two of the aircraft brought their bombs back but the cause was found to be easily remedied by a slight adjustment on the bomb doors. At the close of operations for the day, it was felt that the squadron was at last back into the war.

The success of the day was repeated on 28 December. Both morning and afternoon raids were a huge triumph and all the aircraft returned safely. Again, marshalling yards were the target. The greater success of this operation fell to 'B' flight as through no fault of their own, 'A' flight completely missed the target. Apparently their bombing was compromised by other aircraft attacking on the same course as theirs. This was contrary to briefing instructions and resulted in a curt and very blunt signal to the commanding officer of the squadron concerned.

And so December closed. Quite a frustrating month even though a lot of success was achieved. The Operations Record Book recorded the events of the month in a not too descriptive manner:

End of December—At the beginning of the month the squadron was at Perugia but a move to Cesenatico began on 3rd December, thus bringing the long drawn out training period to a close.

It should be remembered that it was originally estimated that the minimum number of flying days required for the conversion to the Baltimore would be 25. The stay at Perugia was short due to the fact that this aerodrome was extremely unsuitable for training. The three reasons were the runway was too short for beginners, weather would not be good at this time owing to its geographical position and there was no bombing range in existence in that particular area.

John Thompson's diary recalled the month in a far more vivid way:

*Above left:* 500 Squadron bomb Conegliano. (*J. Thompson*)

*Above right:* 'C' Charlie bombing—Flt Sgt Thurnham and crew. (*J. Thompson*)

500 Squadron ground crews at Cesenatico, 1945. (*G. Cardew*)

31st December—The blow came today. Had a phone call from engineer officer this morning. Five of my best lads are to be posted away to make way for some 608 squadron lads. I feel very depressed, almost heart-broken in fact. These lads have been very good friends of mine since I have been on 'B' flight. After a very frustrating year this is the last straw. This service life begins to bind on me!

Tents in the snow, Cesenatico, January 1945. (*G. Cardew*)

500 Squadron air crews at Cesenatico, 1945. (*A. D. Cummings*)

# 13

# Baltimore Days

The last year of war arrived on a Monday and dawned bright and chilly. The squadron, in spite of hangovers, were at dawn readiness in preparation for the days operations. Orders had been received to attack anything that moved in enemy territory. Barges, trains, convoys, were all to receive the attention of the Royal Air Force.

January got off to a good start with both 'A' and 'B' flights getting the maximum amount of Baltimores airborne. A fighter escort was provided for this raid, it being in the centre of enemy occupied country. No Luftwaffe were encountered in the event and the target, a military installation, was successfully attacked. One incident did however mar the success. Baltimore 'H' for Harry was shot down by flak near the target. The pilot was Sergeant Frost and it apparently sustained a direct hit whilst still in formation. Losing height and hoping for a soft crash landing, the Baltimore was hit a second time on the way down. It was assumed that Sergeant Frost himself had been injured at the controls for the aircraft was seen to turn over on its back and dive vertically into the ground, the bombs exploding on impact. It was impossible for any member of the crew to have survived such an explosion and the event was mourned by the entire squadron. The afternoon sortie was cancelled at the last minute due to the deterioration of the weather.

The second day saw operations take place in both morning and afternoon. Towards the end of the day when the Baltimores were due back at Cesenatico, the wind changed and a gale blew up. Arriving over their home field, the aircraft saw that a very strong wind was blowing and that the watch tower was busy firing off red 'verey' lights. The flight commander was told that conditions were dangerous at the base and that the squadron was to divert to Iesi. Unfortunately Flight Lieutenant Dolan had received a hit on the port side and had to make an emergency landing come what may. Holding off until the very last minute before contacting the ground and keeping an eye on the windsock at the side of the runway, he landed successfully.

In the early evening amid whoops of joy, some of the ground crews rolled out of Cesenatico for a trip to Iesi to service the aircraft ready for the next day's operations. With a promise of a good meal and bags of wine *en route*, there was no shortage of volunteers.

The next morning all the Baltimores returned safely to Cesenatico, albeit rather muddy from the wet surface at Iesi. Immediately on landing, the remaining ground crews checked and bombed-up the aircraft ready for the afternoon's sorties.

Only one aircraft remained non-serviceable for the afternoon operation. This was 'R' for Roger and it caused many red faces when it was found that it was the one aircraft that had remained at Cesenatico throughout the traumas of the past few days.

The next morning, Thursday, a vicious frost settled throughout the area. The morning operations were hampered by aircraft refusing to start. In the event 'B' flight could only manage four and 'A' flight five aircraft. The afternoon sortie turned out to be something rather special, as John Thompson's diary records:

> After lunch had a special rush job getting off six aircraft detailed to attack von Kesselring's headquarters. Flight Sergeant Newton led with Thomas as observer. We had to do a nippy retraction test on 'S' as it had an undercarriage hang-up.
>
> A Baltimore of 454 squadron pranged badly at the far end of the runway. The aircraft was badly smashed but we understand the crews all got away OK.
>
> Well, all the aircraft got away to give Kesselring his headache. 'R', with Flight Sergeant Stepney, came panicking back early with its bombs still on. The aircraft was badly holed all round as the reception had been rather hot. One piece came in through the pilot's windshield, tearing the screen, smashing the compass and knocking the pilot's 'flak' cap off. It then went straight through the starboard sliding window! All aircraft landed safely and 'O' for orange got off the lightest. There were no casualties but all the machines were well peppered. They looked very battle-scarred!

This was one of the more important targets that the squadron were detailed to attack. Field Marshal Albert von Kesselring held the title of Supreme Commander in Italy. With his headquarters just inside enemy territory it seemed incomprehensible that it would not be attacked by the RAF. It was good fortune that the honour(?) should fall to 500 Squadron.

The operation was led by Flight Sergeant Newton. All the aircraft with the exception of 'R' carried out a successful attack and returned safely to base. All the aircraft were badly holed and required a lot of attention for the next batch of operations. The only detraction from the success of the operation was that it was later verified that Kesselring was not at home!

For the next few days the weather prevented further sorties. This gave the hard pressed ground crews an opportunity to make the battle-scarred aircraft airworthy once again. It was not until the 11th that operations were able to resume. John Thompson's diary:

> 11th Thursday—Still very cold but not so cold as yesterday. Was on early turn—had quite a bit of trouble starting up the lorry, it boiled over due to a frozen radiator. Managed to get all the aircraft running with a little trouble on 'U' and 'T'.

The sortie was against Castel Franconovito. It was a very impressive sight to see the whole wing flying in boxes of six with the faithful Spitfires in close attendance. Raid reasonably successful but all of 'A' flight's formation were badly shot up. Unfortunately for us we had nine serviceable aircraft, so we had to lend 'A' flight two as they are having a run of bad luck. The two aircraft we lent them, 'T' and 'X' were both shot up. 'X' had its mainplanes so damaged it had to go to the central servicing unit. Flight Sergeant Thurnham put up a good show by carrying on to the target after being hit—he smacked the target for an apple and flew back on one engine, making a smashing landing—well done!

Flight Sergeant Littler had his pitot head [*the instrument that gives the air speed indicator reading*] shot away and flew back with another aircraft to give him a guide as to his airspeed. He also had to land 'J' on one engine as the flak had hit his oil cooler and the engine had seized up, the push rods were sticking out everywhere. We got away just after five. Called in the mess for a drink or two and was a little late for bed—ho hum, what a life!

On Friday 12 January, it snowed heavily laying a carpet of white across the whole area. It was not sufficient to prevent local flying and some gun practice but operations against the enemy were cancelled.

With the change in weather, it was not long before someone came up with the idea of brushing paraffin all over the aircraft at night to prevent the frost from lying heavily on them. The idea was to leave it on overnight and wash it off with petrol the next morning, drying the aircraft thoroughly. Needless to say it did not create much of an impression with the hard pressed ground crews who would of course be burdened with the job!

The next few days saw no operations at all. With rain, snow and freezing hail falling constantly, visibility was at zero. On the afternoon of the 17th the weather lifted temporarily and six aircraft took off at 14.35 hours for a raid on some train sidings. All the aircraft returned safely albeit with a few holes in 'V' and 'R'.

The next day with better weather promised, the squadron undertook a new training role, that of blind bombing using radar and VHF. Many of the squadron realised that this was in preparation for a new type of operation, night flying and bombing targets by instruments only.

During the afternoon a little excitement took place on the airfield when a Kittyhawk and a Thunderbolt landed, very badly shot up. The crews were unhurt but both aircraft had to remain at Cesenatico for vital repairs. The American aircraft proved of great interest to all and a pleasant few hours were spent chatting to the American crews.

With cloud breaking fast, Baltimores 'N', 'V', 'T' and 'Q' took off just after midday for a raid into Yugoslavia. After a successful operation, the aircraft landed back at Cesenatico and were immediately refuelled in readiness for another operation.

Cesanetico airstrip, March 1945.
(*G. H. Templeman*)

The second sortie took off, the previous aircraft being accompanied by 'S', 'U', 'R' and 'J'. The ground crews were warned that the target was a sticky one and that the aircraft might return badly damaged. When they circled the airfield on their return, it was obvious that this had been the case.

'U' landed and turned straight off the runway. The emergency tender rushed to the aircraft and found that Pilot Officer Cook, the gunner, had been shot in the legs. Releasing him gently from the confines of the turret, the ambulance men whisked him away to the medical bay. The aircraft itself was in a sorry state. Badly holed and with much of the port wing shot away, it was surprising that it had even flown back. Another bad casualty in 'B' flight was 'R'. This aircraft, whilst not having any casualties to the crew, appeared worse than 'U'. The nose of the aircraft had received a direct hit and the tailplane was barely visible. The belly was badly shot up and one of the oleo legs had collapsed under the strain of the landing.

'A' flight had also received a fair share of damage. With every aircraft holed, 'S' had to be returned to the main servicing unit 'looking like a colander!' Flight Lieutenant Davis was seen to go down in 'J' after a direct hit by flak but he and his crew were later heard to have survived a crash landing. After this holocaust, all operations ceased at 17.00 hours for the day.

January rolled on into February. The weather remained changeable with periodic thick snow covering the aircraft and tented accommodation. With the advent of the new month, the squadron took on a new type of bombing, that of dropping leaflets over enemy territory. The message pointed out to the enemy the futility of continuing the war when so many cities and so much ground had fallen to the Allies. With the tremendous push now taking place in Italy it was felt that the Germans and Italians might just be pushed into surrender. With this in mind, the leaflets read:

IN NORTH ITALY ON VARIOUS ROADS TO THE BRENNER PASS ALLIED FIGHTER PLANES DESTROYED 750 ENGINES AND 2,500 RAILWAY CARRIAGES BELONGING TO THE GERMANS IN THE LAST 3 MONTHS. DURING THESE MONTHS NO ONE COULD AT ANY TIME TRAVEL BY RAIL BETWEEN ITALY AND GERMANY WITHOUT INTERRUPTION EITHER AROUND THE BRENNER PASS OR ALONG THE UDINE LINE. MORE THAN HALF THE TIME THE PASSING THROUGH WAS IMPOSSIBLE BECAUSE OF THE DESTROYED BRIDGES OVER THE RIVERS ETSCH, BRENTA, LIVENZA, THE PIAVE AND THE TAGLIAMENTO.

THESE TRUE STORIES, GERMAN SOLDIERS, ARE COMING VERY CLOSE TO YOU, THE TIME IS COMING WHEN YOUR LEADERS WILL TRY TO PULL OUT OF ITALY SO THAT YOU CAN BE SENT TO THE EAST OR WEST FRONT. THE WHOLE OF THE ALLIED AIR FORCE IN ITALY, WHICH AT THE MOMENT IS BOMBING PLACES IN AUSTRIA AND GERMANY, WILL BE TURNING ON YOU IN THE TOWNS OF VERONA, ALA, LAVIS, SAN MICHELE AND TRIENT, TURNING THE ROADS INTO A BLOODY MESS. THINK, GERMAN SOLDIERS IN ITALY, WHEN THE ORDER FOR THE RETURN NORTH IS GIVEN, STAY BEHIND. THE ITALIAN PEOPLE WILL HELP YOU HIDE AND WAIT FOR OUR ARRIVAL. WE TOLD YOU EARLIER ON AND ARE TELLING YOU AGAIN YOUR ONLY SURE WAY OF GETTING HOME WILL BE THROUGH THE ALLIED PRISONER OF WAR CAMPS.

On the other side of the leaflet was a map showing the danger route to the Brenner Pass.

Another new type of operation about this time was the introduction of night bombing raids over enemy territory. This was hoped to reduce the number of losses and the amount of damage done to our aircraft during the daytime operations.

On Friday 2 February 1945, news was received that the Russians were within 35 miles of Berlin. Amid much whooping and many cheers it was felt that at last the end was in sight. The news was celebrated in the evening by a free mess for the airmen.

Whenever the weather relented, operations were now continuing by day and night, much to the disgust of the ground crews who had their work load almost doubled. The night targets turned out to be very similar to those of the day. Railways, military installations and German strongholds, all were attacked, the crews now flying with the aid of radar and illumination of the targets by flares.

By day, many of the operations were deep into Yugoslavia. The Partisans and Resistance groups that were organised all over the country needed to be supplied with food and arms to enable them to continue the fight against the Germans. Apart from attacking the enemy in Yugoslavia, it fell to the squadron to make many supply drops to the patriots.

March proved to be a little better for the squadron. With the weather settling down a little, it was apparent that there was to be no let-up in these last few months of war. The news from all quarters was very good. The enemy was retreating in every field of the war and the Russians were definitely within walking distance of Berlin. At Cesenatico, the arrival of American Thunderbolts to push the war even faster in our favour caused a great deal of excitement. The airfield was becoming a home for several nationalities and air forces. With far faster and larger aircraft being stationed there, it necessitated much upheaval for the resident squadrons. The runway had to be widened and several of the accommodation areas had to be moved, including that of 500 Squadron. This entailed the temporary closure of the airmen's mess amid cries of dismay and anger. It was however short-lived and in no time at all the bars were back in business with a far better selection of alcohol—much of it American—than ever before.

By 24 March, the Americans were on operations. They announced their arrival in the theatre by dropping a bomb on the canal at Cesenatico, killing a soldier and then promptly crashing on the runway, the Thunderbolt breaking into a million pieces. This did not go down too well with the men of 500 Squadron, their tents were in a direct line with the end of the runway!

The next day saw the Americans carrying out the maximum number of operations with the maximum number of aircraft. Not so 'A' and 'B' flights of 500 whose Baltimores were beginning to feel the strain of constant battle. A reduced number of aircraft were sent on the day's operation, a raid on a bridge over one of the numerous rivers of the region. All machines did however return safely and relatively unscathed, allowing the work on the remainder of the aircraft to be completed.

March closed with a visit from the Archbishop of York, Dr Garbett, who gave the squadron a very interesting talk. He brought a lot of long awaited news from home and returned to England with bundles of letters for the loved ones back there. With the war evidently in its last few months, he not only acted as an envoy to the men but his presence was of great encouragement in this, the final push.

And the last push it most certainly was. On 30 March the Russians captured Danzig and the second Ukrainian front opened its offensive. The next day the United States 1st and 9th Armies completed their encirclement of the Ruhr, linking up at Lippstadt thus preventing munitions and steel leaving the Ruhr factories.

By 10 April, the United States 9th Army had taken the German city of Hanover and the British 2nd Army crossed the Leine and cut the Hamburg to Hanover road. With rapid progress the Russians took Vienna at the same time that the British and American troops reached and liberated the death camps at Belsen and Buchenwald. Arnhem in Holland was taken on 15 April and the rest of the month saw success after success for the Allies.

Despite the obvious decline in the war, 500 Squadron was still very much in the operational role. John Thompson's diary:

> Friday 13th. Up nice and early today feeling just a shade liverish. Got all the aircraft off without any trouble. I am on duty all night so stayed up at the camp after lunch,

sunbathing and reading. Have just been informed that there are ten sorties on tonight.

22.00 hrs. Night flying went off OK with exception of 'X' which had an electrical failure. Flying Officer Cresswell had to take an 'A' flight aircraft which didn't suit him any too well. We ended up doing nine sorties and I went back to the tent soon after 07.30.

The operations were, however, short-lived. With the capture of Mussolini near the Swiss border on 28 April and his subsequent death at the hands of Italian partisans, the number of targets to be hit dwindled. The next day representatives of the German Army agreed to sign an unconditional surrender at Caserta, and hostilities ceased on 2 May.

Realising that the end was near, Adolf Hitler nominated Admiral Dönitz as his successor and immediately married Eva Braun, his mistress. The marriage was short, the next day they committed suicide together in a sitting room of the bunker, she by biting into a capsule of cyanide and he by shooting himself. The Italian Campaign finished on 1 May 1945. For 500 Squadron it meant the end of a hard and gruelling campaign that had lasted for a year and a half. It had cost the squadron many lives and much anguish. It had also brought them recognition for a job done well and the majority of the men felt that it was indeed a job well done. The 500 diarist recorded on 1 May:

> As the war in Italy is drawing to a close, the wing could not find any targets for the squadron. The Italian Campaign ended with the surrender of the German and Italian forces. News was received quietly without the expected scenes of jubilation. Air Vice Marshal A. E. Borton CB, CMG, DSO, AFC, the Kent Regional Liaison Officer today visited the squadron auxiliaries.

Flight Sergeant John Thompson wrote:

> The pace quickens on the last downhill glide to Victory—and what? Armistice is expected hourly but the grim struggle in Berlin and Czechoslovakia goes on. Here in Italy things are almost at a standstill. No targets and to cap it all, the weather has deteriorated badly and we are getting heavy showers and thunderstorms. Have had several good 'drunks' in the mess with the boys but the general atmosphere seems a little strained and the jollity rather forced. Decided to go on leave to Rome tomorrow—might as well grab it while I can.

The last few operations took place in the vicinity of the Po Valley. The great river that wound its way across the country would have provided the Germans with a way of escape during the hours of darkness. Flying by instruments at night, the squadron kept up a constant bombardment over the area thus ensuring the Germans did not use the river.

Bailey bridge across the Po. (*G. Cardew*)

The County of Kent Regional Liaison Officer, Air Vice Marshal Borton, on his visit to the squadron, found a very anxious and excited 500. Anxious to hear news of the families at home and excited that at last it appeared to be nearly over. The Air Vice Marshal brought a message from the Right Honourable Anthony Eden, who had just assumed the post of Honorary Air Commodore, to the squadron following the death, on active service, of His Royal Highness the Duke of Kent in a Sunderland flying boat crash. His message read:

> I have just received your telegram and am deeply touched by its terms. I can assure you that I am proud of the honour that you have conferred upon me. I congratulate all ranks most warmly on their splendid record and look forward to an opportunity to visit them and thank them in person. Good luck—Anthony Eden.

Although the war in Europe was now officially over and there were no real targets for the squadron, training still continued at a rapid pace. No official orders had as yet been received as to where or what the squadron was to do at the conclusion and so something of an anti-climax set in.

A Victory night party was held in all three messes on 3 May and free drinks were served until the early hours of the morning. The duty air and ground crews awoke next morning with not only throbbing heads but also the realisation that peace was here!

Winston Churchill and Harry S. Truman proclaimed the 8 May VE day, the Germans had finally decided to capitulate in Prague. VE day or not, the following signal was received at Cesenatico for the attention of the Commanding Officer 500 Squadron: '500 Squadron to proceed immediately to Villa Orba. The movement is to be carried out with the utmost speed and efficiency.'

And this on a day of celebration, surely it must be a bad joke! Yet no, the signal was authentic and the squadron diarist recorded:

500 Squadron cross the River Po, 16 May 1945. (*G. Cardew*)

All our hopes were rudely shattered on VE day when we were ordered to move out with the utmost celerity to Villa Orba. Preparations were duly started and a party set out next morning for the new base.

The airfield at Villa Orba was situated near the town of Udine just on the Yugoslavian border. It was a pretty little airfield compared with the normal site in Italy. With summer fast approaching it was an idyllic situation for the squadron. Regular bathing parties were organised and everyone took this last opportunity to tan himself. The motto was: 'If we are going home after all this time we may as well go home with a tan.'

With no operations planned, flying training filled in the time until the total world war ended. New exercises included photographic and air firing at a towed air drogue. One highlight of May was when the Desert Air Force held a Victory flypast. The Baltimores of 500 Squadron led No. 253 wing in the formation of aircraft that overflew some of the airfields, towns and headquarters in celebration.

The exercises embraced aircraft detection and fighter control and many cross-country flights. On 1 June 1945, Flight Lieutenant Hide and his crew intercepted the Royal Navy cruisers *Ajax* and *Achilles* and escorted them into Trieste harbour. This enabled the crews of the ships to engage in some fighter control practice. It seemed as though since the war had ended, the authorities had begun a hard campaign of training. Army, Navy and Air Force were all thrown into a strict routine.

Nissen hut accommodation, Villa-Orba, 1945. (*G. H. Templeman*)

The interior for 500 Squadron. (*G. H. Templeman*)

Airmen's billets Italian style.

Detachment of 500 passing a landslide in Italy.

Medical site and tented accommodation for 500 Squadron, Villa-Orba, Italy. (*G. H. Templeman*)

Medical section for the Squadron.

## Baltimore Days

Further excitement came to Villa Orba on 2 June. Three days before, Flight Lieutenant Mason and his crew had taken off from the base on a communications sortie in one of the Baltimores. They were overdue back at base, and no radio signal having been received at Villa Orba, it was assumed they had crashed. A search of the route they had taken was made by other aircraft of the squadron but this proved nothing and they were accordingly posted as missing.

Early in the morning of the 2nd a twin engined aircraft was heard approaching Villa Orba. As it got nearer the aircraft was recognised as a Baltimore, but whose? No aircraft had taken off as yet that morning. Lowering its wheels, the Baltimore turned into a perfect landing and rolled to a halt at the dispersal area. The serial number of the aircraft could now be seen and as though returned from the dead, it was Flight Lieutenant Mason. Wing Commander Garbett met the men off the aircraft and slowly the remarkable story unfolded.

The aircraft had taken off on the original sortie in clear weather. One hour into the flight, the cloud had thickened and the crew was forced to rely on instrument flying. Unfortunately, and unknown to Flight Lieutenant Mason, the compass was faulty and was taking them off course. So far off in fact, that they had inadvertently crossed the Russian line and Russian radar had picked them up on their screens. Six Russian fighters suddenly appeared beside them and, by sign language, one of the crews indicated that the Baltimore was to follow them.

Villa-Orba airfield, Italy 1945. (G. H. Templeman)

Fifteen minutes later they landed at the Russian held airfield of Graz where, they were immediately taken captive and were detained for three days in cells for interrogation. The Russians finally accepted their story, repaired the faulty compass and released the crew. They then escorted them to the edge of the Russian zone before finally leaving the Baltimore on its own. This explained the absence of any radio signal or notification of the aircraft's fate.

The whole incident was officially put down as a misunderstanding and a lack of co-operation by the Russians. Months after the war had ended, it was regarded as the first warning and foretaste of things to come when dealing with the Russians.

And so the month of June came to its conclusion. Not a very significant month as the Operations Record Book recorded:

> Villa Orba—summary of June. Throughout this month training flying has been carried out successfully by all aircrew. This has embraced solo navigational and photographic exercises, air firing and formation flying.

July was even briefer:—'Villa Orba—summary of July. Flying training.' The men of the squadron were now very impatient to pack up and go home. They could not see the object of constant training when there was no enemy to attack. The squadron still carried out its vital task as a link with bases throughout Europe until Transport Command took over the duties halfway through July. Then nothing. The weather was hot and sultry and to cap it all, on the 22 July, the very popular commanding officer, Wing Commander Garbet received notification of his posting to attend a course at the Royal Air Force staff college which was then at Gerrards Cross. Addressing the squadron for the last time, he thanked the men for their support and the magnificent achievements of the squadron whilst under his command. He was given a typical rousing send-off and flew out leaving many memories.

July became August and still no mention of postings back home. Flying training still continued until, when it was felt no more could be endured, the magical signal arrived. It was all over. It was time to leave this foreign land and go home.

# 14

# Peacetime Operations

Here is the six o'clock news for today August 6th. It is announced from the White House that at noon today, an atomic bomb was dropped over the ancient Japanese city of Hiroshima. Wide devastation has been caused and the city and surrounding area is in flames and ruin. The aircraft returned safely to base.

With this cold announcement came a new concept of aerial warfare and warfare in general. The dropping of an atomic device on a city heralded a new and far more lethal way of conducting war. It would never be the same again.

On 9 August, another device was detonated above the Japanese city of Nagasaki. Again total destruction was obtained and it was this final death blow that brought the world war to a close. On 14 August Japan surrendered.

The signal announcing the end of all hostilities came the next day when Winston Churchill proclaimed it VJ day. Everybody began to rejoice.

At Villa Orba the signal was received with heartfelt thanks. The 500 Squadron diarist recorded:

The world war is ended. The Japanese formally surrendered this morning. Today and tomorrow have been declared holidays except for those on essential work.

Finally the long years of conflict had come to an end. To some present it felt like an anti-climax, to others it just did not seem possible that the war had finally come to an end. Thoughts went back to past events, many who had died or been injured and maimed in the cause of freedom were affectionately remembered and mourned by their comrades still living. Now was the time for the remaining members of the squadron to wipe the sweat from their brows and the moisture from their eyes and consider if the grim struggle had been really worthwhile.

After VJ day the intense training programme came to an end. It was hoped that the squadron would be returned home as quickly as possible. On 23 August 1945, during a violent thunderstorm accompanied by torrential rain, the Air Officer Commanding

Desert Air Force Air Vice Marshal Whitford paid a farewell visit to the squadron. In his speech he congratulated the entire squadron on its decisive part in the defeat of the enemy and praised the squadron's efficiency. He then gave the news that the present 500 Squadron was to be posted to Eastleigh in Kenya and would be renumbered No. 249 (Gold Coast) Squadron Royal Air Force. This was necessary to keep in use the number of the fighter squadron in which the late Wing Commander J. B. Nicholson, the former Tonbridge schoolboy, had gained Fighter Command's only Victoria Cross on 16 August 1940. After thanking 500 Squadron for all its sterling work the AOC stated that the auxiliary airmen would be sent back to England, and that, with effect from midnight 23 August, 500 Squadron would be reformed at Maidstone in Kent.

Towards the end of August as the auxiliaries were preparing to leave Villa Orba for home, Wing Commander Matson arrived to take the remainder of the squadron to Eastleigh. This move marked the end of the long and cherished wartime career of 500 Squadron. But now the peacetime structure of the forces was being forged and the Air Ministry, in their wisdom, decided that the country could not do without an auxiliary air force.

And so, in June 1946, a new 500 Squadron began to form at West Malling fighter station in Kent as a night fighter unit equipped with the de Havilland Mosquito NF 30 aircraft. The Mosquito had proved a very tough and aggressive fighter-bomber in the latter years of the war and a mark of the aircraft had now been designed for night fighter duties.

The first commanding officer of peacetime was Squadron Leader Patrick Green, OBE, AFC. He had served in 500 Squadron from 1936 to 1940 and was no stranger to many of the former auxiliary airmen who had re-enlisted in the squadron.

Training on the Mosquito began almost immediately although the peacetime auxiliaries really only came into their own from Friday until Sunday. The training

Mosquitoes at West Malling 1946–47. (*G. Cardew*)

had such good results that Squadron Leader Green was able to take the squadron to summer camp at Tangmere in 1947.

500 Squadron was of course no stranger to Tangmere. It was the first camp ever attended by the auxiliaries way back in 1933. It had risen to become a prominent base during the war and was now a major peacetime airfield. With glorious summer weather and the promise of much flying from an airfield surrounded by many orchards, it was no wonder that the squadron achieved almost a hundred per cent attendance at camp.

Upon arrival back at West Malling after a successful two weeks the command of the squadron passed to Squadron Leader H. C. Kennard, DFC. This officer arrived at the same time as a directive sent by the Air Ministry stating that all auxiliary squadrons were to become day fighter squadrons.

Squadron Leader Kennard had flown with 66 squadron during the Battle of Britain and later with 610 (County of Chester), 306 (Polish) and 121 (Eagle) squadrons, of which he was the commanding officer. He had the pleasure of telling the squadron that it would be the first auxiliary squadron to receive jet powered aircraft.

On 14 August 1948 the squadron received the first of the Gloster Meteor Mk.F3. Powered by two Rolls Royce Welland jet engines developing a thrust of 1,700 lb, the Meteor was in fact the first allied aircraft powered by a jet engine to see action in the war. It was a fast single seat fighter capable of reaching a speed of 410 mph at 30,000 feet. It was fitted with four 20 mm guns, and the squadron gladly exchanged the Mosquito for this modern aircraft.

Annual camp that year was held at Thorney Island in Hampshire. During the first week the squadron was visited by the Honorary Air Commodore of the squadron, Mr Anthony Eden. Taking a great interest in the new aircraft he started up the jet

Meteor Mk.7 and Mk.8s at West Malling 1952. (*Kent Messenger*)

engines of a Meteor and upon stepping down announced to the world's press that it was absolutely incredible. Accompanied by his son Nicholas, Mr Eden saw all aspects of the squadron's work and met many of the men. In his speech he stated that the squadron's strength now stood at 21 officers and 41 non-commissioned officers and airmen and that this really was a magnificent achievement. At the end of his stay with them, many members of the squadron visited him at his home in Havant near Thorney Island.

Again in 1949 two weeks' training was held at Thorney Island. Continuing their training throughout the year the squadron was rewarded for its efforts during the early part of 1950 when the Mk.3 Meteor was exchanged for the Mk.4. The newer mark of aircraft had the more powerful Rolls Royce Derwent engines giving a greater performance and pushing the thrust up to 3,500 lb. This same mark of Meteor did in fact raise the world speed record to 616 mph on 7 September 1946.

It did not take the squadron long to adjust to the Meteor Mk.4. Summer camp was once again spent at Thorney Island, the aircraft flying directly to the airfield leaving the remainder of the squadron to travel by train on 13 August.

Anthony Eden once more paid the squadron a visit. It was always pleasant to see him as he took such an active interest in every aspect of the squadron's training.

War reared its ugly head once again in 1951 when the Korean crisis erupted. In common with all other auxiliary units, 500 Squadron was called up for three to six months' full time active service. It was not known at this time just what course of action the war would take; hence the squadron's being at readiness. The last three weeks of the call up were spent back again at Tangmere. When it was evident that the situation was not as bad as originally envisaged, the squadron was stood down and the men returned to West Malling to carry on their duties as weekend airmen.

In 1952, the squadron exchanged its Mk.4s for the new Meteor Mk.8. With the new aircraft came a Mk.7 trainer. The performance of the aircraft had again improved and it was now capable of 590 mph. The Mk.7 allowed many of the ground crews to experience a flight with the squadron. Certain rules however had to be obeyed. G. L. Clinch remembers:

> One weekend at West Malling I was asked if I would like a flight in the Meteor 7. Of course I jumped at the chance. The fitter that was standing by said: 'If you are sick you clean the cockpit out yourself.' In spite of this warning, I still went up.
>
> The flight was absolutely grand. We did every kind of aerobatic trick that there was. Whilst we were on the top of a loop, I noticed that the undercarriage warning lamp came on. When we landed I reported the unlocking of the undercarriage to the engineering officer. Just a couple of weeks later there was a directive from the Ministry stating that Meteor Mk.7s were not, repeat not, to do aerobatics. I like to think that this was the result of my report. I am glad to say that I was not sick either!

Annual inspection at West Malling 1951. (*Kent Messenger*)

The squadron at Thorney Island summer camp, 1949–50. Anthony Eden in centre with Squadron Leader Kennard on his left. (*Evening News and Hampshire Telegraph*)

Anthony Eden at Thorney Island, 1950. (*Evening News and Hampshire Telegraph*)

Anthony Eden made regular trips to West Malling to see the squadron and he himself flew in the Mk.7 occasionally. The squadron had the honour to escort Mr Eden in May 1952 when he was Foreign Minister. Four Meteors rendezvoused with his official aircraft over France and escorted him back from Paris to London.

The year also saw the command of the squadron pass to Squadron Leader Desmond de Villiers AFC. He had joined 500 Squadron in the post war period, as a junior officer, after flying with a number of squadrons during the Second World War. He was employed as a test pilot for de Havilland. The opportunity to take command of an auxiliary squadron came as a welcome break from the rigours of test flying.

The annual two week camp in 1952 was held at Leuchars in Fife. This was a very prominent Fighter Command base and it allowed the auxiliaries every opportunity to compete with the regular units stationed there. This increased the amount of friendly rivalry between them and any little incident would give one unit the edge on the other. G. L. Clinch remembers:

> One day at Leuchars we were detailed to carry out a daily inspection on one of the Meteors. For some unknown reason, it was carried out on the wrong aircraft. It wasn't until we saw the plane moving out of the dispersal area that we realised why. As the plane came towards us, the nose wheel door carried the code 'E'. As it turned and passed us we saw that the rudder was coded 'C'.
>
> Of course, every auxiliary airman had the answer to the officer who threatened to put him on a charge! It was: 'You charge me and I'll go home.' This was the only occasion that I can remember that the laugh was on us auxiliaries and the regulars never let us forget it.

One particular feature that gave 500 Squadron an air of superiority over many of the auxiliary squadrons was when, with the authority of the local councils, each Meteor carried the crest and name of a particular town in Kent. Each pilot was undoubtedly proud of his own aircraft but when the aircraft were all parked line abreast at dispersal, the impact of this was immediately seen.

Many 'dining in' evenings were once again held at Astley House, the old training hall, now that the squadron were resident at West Malling. The house had not changed much since the early dark days of 1938–39 when Ann Griffiths and the rest of the men and women of the auxiliaries had trained for what eventually turned out to be six years of war. The spirit was the same as in those days, only time had changed. Exuberance still abounded, as Group Captain D. M. Candler recalls:

> We used to have very good 'dining in' nights at Astley House. The men, I remember, at one time clubbed together to buy a piano that one of them had seen. It cost the princely sum of £5 0s 0d and many thought it would be nice to have a piano in the mess for social evenings.

# Peacetime Operations

Meteors over Kent. (*Russell Adams*)

Fine formation of No. 500.

Meteor Mk.8, West Malling 1956. (*G. Cardew*)

Pilot Officer Dave Croucher in Meteor Mk.8, West Malling 1955–56. (*Dave Croucher*)

AOCs inspection, West Malling. (*G. Cardew*)

However, not everyone thought alike. Their intention was that the piano should not be played. With a sound like charging Indians, several of the officers descended on this poor piano with axes, hammers and all manner of dreadful weapons. In no time at all the poor piano was demolished and lying in pieces on the mess floor. As if this was not enough, it was then burnt ceremoniously in the officers mess grate.

People walking along the Hastings road just outside Astley House were horrified to see great clouds of black smoke emitting from one of the chimneys. Slowly this cloud sank back to earth and enveloped the residents within 200 yards in all directions. The next mess evening, many complaints were read out concerning the damage to washing that had been put out to dry that very evening and next morning was found to be covered in soot and wood flakes.

In 1953 the squadron attended summer camp at Takali in Malta. For obvious reasons this proved to be a very popular camp and the attendance was almost one hundred per cent. The administration and ground crews were flown out by Transport Command, the Meteors being flown out by their pilots. With the temperature well into the nineties, shorts were the order of the day. With the ideal climate the squadron was able to fly the maximum number of hours and although everyone ensured that they had a good time whilst on the island, the camp turned out to be a first class training period for both air and ground crews.

A very tanned and healthy squadron returned to West Malling at the end of the two week period. The Meteors had been able to get in some first class gunnery practise whilst in the Mediterranean, the climate allowing a very good vision when firing at a ground target.

A new commanding officer arrived in 1954. Squadron Leader D. M. Clause AFC relieved Desmond de Villiers and at the same time Flight Lieutenant Bonney, a former aircraft apprentice who had flown Spitfires and Thunderbolts in the Far East, arrived to take the position of squadron adjutant.

Summer camp was again held at Takali and many members of the squadron had the opportunity of meeting the radio and television personality Jeanne Heal, when she was hosting and presenting a show from Malta. The show was entitled 'Meet Jeanne Heal'.

1954 was also a significant year for the squadron, when they won the coveted 'Cooper' trophy. This was an annual award given to the auxiliary squadron which, in the eyes of the Ministry, had shown the greatest overall efficiency throughout the year. It was received by Squadron Leader Clause during an official ceremony.

In 1955 command of the squadron passed to Squadron Leader D. H. M. Candler who came to 500 from the then Central Fighter Establishment at West Raynham in Norfolk. The squadron was back at Takali for camp when it was announced, amid great jubilation, that this year the squadron had been awarded the 'Esher' trophy for operational efficiency throughout the year.

Malta, 1951. 'Part-time' airmen at camp. (*Kent Messenger*)

Squadron Leader De Villiers in his Meteor 8 cockpit, Malta, 1953.

West Malling 1955–56. Dave Morris and Norman Hutchings above, Dave Croucher below. (*D. Croucher*)

## Peacetime Operations

The squadron meets Jeanne Heal at Malta camp, 1954. (*Kent Messenger*)

The squadron leave for two weeks training in Malta. Mayor of Maidstone (Alderman A. H. Clark) giving a send-off, 1954. (*Kent Messenger*)

Pilots and ground crew being inspected by Anthony Eden at West Malling, 9 July 1955. (*Kent Messenger*)

Members of the Squadron relax at Malta.

*Above left:* 500 Squadron at West Malling. (*G. Cardew*)

*Above right:* Lord Cornwallis presents the Esher Trophy to Sqn Ldr Candler.

## Peacetime Operations

Meteor Mk 8s in formation.

The Esher Trophy about to be marched into the ranks on 16 Feburary 1957. Bearer Pilot Officer Hubbard, Escort Front Pilot Officer Green, Escort Rear Pilot Officer Hanmore.

Again in 1956, the award of the 'Esher' trophy went to 500 Squadron. The presentation of the trophy by Anthony Eden to Squadron Leader Candler was enhanced by the squadron's twenty-fifth anniversary celebrations.

On 11 August 1956, the squadron was greatly honoured by receiving the Freedom of the Borough of Maidstone. A parade and march past through the centre of the county town marked the honour whilst the Meteors of 500 flew over County Hall in salute. With bayonets fixed and standards flying, the men of the squadron turned in salute as they passed the Town Hall.

The squadron was adopted by the Borough of Folkestone on 3 October and at a dinner at Astley House, A. V. Roe Ltd, who had made the Ansons which the squadron had flown early in the war, presented a model of the aircraft made in solid silver. It was received by Squadron Leader Candler for the entire squadron.

Sadly the battle honours, the trophies won and the Freedom of the county town did not halt the disbandment of the squadron when, early in 1957, the Air Ministry decided to order all auxiliary units to stand down. It was thought that future wars would not require the manpower that was now available in the Royal Air Force, thus in the interests of national economy the volunteer units were to close.

With the stand down official, 16 February 1957 saw the 'Esher' trophy on show for the last time when it was marched into the ranks at a public ceremony. With Pilot Officer Hubbard bearing the trophy and Pilot Officers Green and Hanimore escorting, it was received within the ranks and was then marched through Maidstone with a final salute being taken at the Town Hall.

In March 1957 500 Squadron was disbanded. The aircraft and other items of equipment went to the regular units or to the scrap heap. The men were allowed to keep only their memories. Squadron Leader Candler told me:

> When the order came to stand down, it numbed the whole of the squadron with shock. After all these post-war years of training and loyalty it appeared as though we were being sent out to graze. Despite many protests and letters to the Ministry, it was all to no avail. The auxiliaries were no longer wanted.
>
> At the last dinner (or supper!) at West Malling, the dinner cards were in black and bore the inscription RIP. It was rather a solemn occasion, enlivened only when a tremendous bang was heard outside the mess. With the mess pictures falling from their hooks, we all went to the main entrance to see a huge fire outside. Sitting in the middle was a car rapidly shrinking. Exuberance had done it again.

And so this time it was final for the squadron. There was no hope of a reprieve. With heavy hearts the squadron disbanded and the part time airmen went to their own walks of life. The Battle Honours awarded to the squadron were the pride of every member. The Channel and the North Sea 1939–41, Dunkirk, Biscay Ports 1941, Atlantic 1941–42, North Africa 1942–43, Mediterranean 1942–444 and Italy 1944–45. None of this could prevent the final judgement.

# Peacetime Operations

The march through Maidstone, 16 February 1957.

Meteors over County Hall, Maidstone, 1956–57. (*Kent Messenger*)

Members of the 500 Old Comrades Association at the Royal Star Hotel, Maidstone, 1959.

A ceremony unique in Royal Air Force history took place at Maidstone Army Barracks on Saturday 21 September 1963. The squadron was remustered for one day to receive the Standard from the Earl of Avon (formally Sir Anthony Eden).

Flying Officer R. de V. Rudolph carried the Standard after its consecration by the Chaplain-in-Chief, Royal Air Force.

It was then received for safe keeping by the Vicar at All Saints Church, Maidstone. A parade was held with a marching contingent from the Queen's Colour Squadron of the Royal Air Force and the Central Band provided the music. Former members of the squadron paraded in civilian clothes, led by Group Captain W. K. LeMay, the commanding officer in 1939–40. Many distinguished guests including Lord Cornwallis, then Lord Lieutenant of Kent, and Air Marshal Douglas Morris attended the ceremony. The official press release from the Air Ministry mentioned the squadron's unofficial Anson fire power modification and stated that it was the leading maritime squadron in the Western Mediterranean, and the most highly decorated. The release ended with the mention that 500 Squadron was the first auxiliary squadron to receive jet powered aircraft.

With this ceremony over, it was left to the historians and the annals of Royal Air Force history to remember and record all that the squadron had achieved during its long history. Many who led it or who served in it have left their mark on military and civil aviation. Air Marshal Sir Patrick Hunter Dunn KBE, CB, DFC, Air Marshal Sir Andrew McKee, KCB, CBE, DSO, DFC, AFC, and Air Chief Marshal Sir Denis Spotswood KCB, CBE, DSO, DFC, to name but a few. There are many others.

The squadron may have disappeared from the Royal Air Force Order of Battle but it will never, never be forgotten.

# Commanding Officers Of 500 Squadron (In Ranks Then Held)

| | |
|---|---|
| Squadron Leader S. R. Watkins AFC | March 1931 |
| Wing Commander L. F. Forbes MC | July 1931 |
| Wing Commander R. Halley DFC | July 1933 |
| Squadron Leader G. M. Lawson MC | May 1935 |
| Flight Lieutenant W. G. Wooliams | April 1936 |
| Squadron Leader G. K. Hohler R. Aux. AF | October 1936 |
| Squadron Leader W. LeMay R. Aux. AF | October 1939 |
| Wing Commander G. H. Turner | June 1940 |
| Wing Commander M. Q. Candler | March 1941 |
| Wing Commander G. T. Gilbert | July 1941 |
| Wing Commander D. F. Spotswood DSO, DFC | April 1942 |
| Wing Commander D. G. Keddie | April 1943 |
| Wing Commander C. K. Bonner | April 1944 |
| Wing Commander C. E. A. Garton | June 1944 |
| Wing Commander H. N. Garbett | July 1944 |
| Wing Commander Matson | August 1945 |
| Squadron Leader P. Green OBE, AFC, R. Aux. AF | August 1946 |
| Squadron Leader M. C. Kennard DFC, R. Aux. AF | February 1949 |
| Squadron Leader D. de Villiers R. Aux. AF | March 1952 |
| Squadron Leader D. M. Clause | August 1954 |
| Squadron Leader D. H. M. Candler | October 1945 to March 1957 |

# No. 500 Squadron Standard

Standards for Royal Air Force squadrons were created by George VI on 1 April 1943 to mark the twenty-fifth anniversary of the formation of the Royal Air Force. A Standard is a fringed and tasselled silken banner mounted on a pike surmounted by a golden eagle and has a decorative border embroidered with the national emblems of the British Isles. In the centre is the squadron badge and to each side of this are white scrolls inscribed with the Battle Honours.

The Battle Honours were earned during the Second World War and represent fields of intensive operations both at home and abroad.

| | |
|---|---|
| Channel and North Sea | 1939–41 Dunkirk |
| Biscay Ports | 1941 |
| Atlantic | 1941–42 |
| North Africa | 1942–43 |
| Mediterranean | 1942–44 |
| Italy | 1944–45 |

Decorations awarded during the 1939–45 war included:

3 DSOs
21 DFCs and one bar to DFC
1 CGM
9 DFMs
25 Mentioned in Despatches

500 (County of Kent) Squadron Royal Auxiliary Air Force
Old Comrades Association

# Squadron Bases

| | |
|---|---|
| Manston | 16 March 1931 |
| Detling | 28 September 1938 |
| Warmwell | 30 July 1939 |
| Detling | 13 August 1939 |
| Bircham Newton | 30 May 1941 |
| Stornaway | 2 April 1942 |
| St Eval | 31 August 1942 |
| Gibraltar | 5 November 1942 |
| Tafaraoui | 3 May 1943 |
| La Senia | 6 January 1944 to 11 July 1944 |
| La Senia | 1 August 1944 |
| Left for Italy | 24 August 1944 |
| Pescara | 14 September 1944 |
| Perugia | 15 October 1944 |
| Cesenatico | 9 December 1944 |
| Villa Orba | 10 May 1945 |
| Eastleigh | 28 September 1945 |
| West Malling | 10 May 1946 to 10 March 1957 |

| Aircraft Equipment | Period of Service | Representative Serial |
|---|---|---|
| Virginia X 'City of Canterbury' | March 1931–January 1936 | J7566 (B) |
| Hart | January 1936–May 1937 | K3018 |
| Hind | February 1937–March 1939 | K6700 |
| Anson 1 | March 1939–April 1941 | N5233 (MK-Q) |
| Blenheim IV | April 1941–November 1941 | Z6050 |
| Hudson III, V | November 1941–April 1944 | FK444 |

| | | |
|---|---|---|
| Ventura V | December 1943–July 1944 | FP633 (MK-R) |
| Baltimore IV, V | September 1944–September 1945 | FA618 (C) |
| Mosquito NF30 | April 1947–October 1948 | NT606 (RAA-H) |
| Meteor F3 | July 1948–October 1951 | EE420 (RAA-B) |
| Meteor F4 | July 1951–February 1952 | VT169 (S7-F) |
| Meteor F8 | November 1951–March 1957 | WF714 (K) |

# Bibliography

*21 Squadrons* — Leslie Hunt
*RAF Biggin Hill* — Graham Wallace
*The War in the Air* — Gavin Lyall
*Fly for your Life* — Larry Forrester
*Duel of Eagles* — Peter Townsend
*Battle over Britain* — Francis K. Mason
*The Big Show* — Pierre Closterman
*Kent Messenger* Photographic Archives